WORLD WAR
C

Select books by PARIS TOSEN

The Science of Reality

The Earth-Colonizing Handbook of Generation Stelan

God is DNA

500 Trillion To One: Odds of Collapsing Three Towers

Persons Artificial: Simulacra at the Wheel of America

WORLD WAR

C

THE SECRET AND DESTRUCTIVE WEATHER WAR BETWEEN RUSSIA AND AMERICA

PARIS TOSEN

CANADA

World War C

Second edition, June 2016
First edition, June 2015

Also published as *Why Malaysia Airlines Flight 370 Vanished* (2016).

This publication is designed to provide advanced and theoretical information in regard to the subject matter covered. This material may not be suitable for everyone. Some errors may exist.

Book and cover design, Paris Tosen

ISBN 978-1-514283-68-4 (pbk)
ISBN 978-1-988014-07-4 (eBook)

www.tosen.ca

Contents

This book describes extreme natural disasters in a way that might offend some readers. The author provides a controversial hypothesis that is still in the very early stages of research and understanding.

Preface

On March 23, 2014 I published the first version of this book under the title *Why Malaysia Airlines Flight 370 Vanished* in electronic format, 14 days after Malaysia Airlines Flight 370 vanished into thin air and well before any significant search and rescue operations had begun. If it wasn't obvious to the reader, it is nearly impossible to write a book, let alone a *good* book, on a subject if the subject hadn't even been properly investigated. To some I might have appeared to be an idiot, a man who jumped to the unobvious conclusion with as much of a radical theory as he could summon. In regards to MH370, this was not the case.

It was not the case because I'm not an idiot nor do I have all the answers all the time. In fact, my discussions tend to take on a very different slant, not because I have a different point of view, rather it is because of the nature of the events I discuss. When the nature of the event, such as the case surrounding the sudden disappearance of a

Boeing 777—a rather large aircraft equipped with millions of dollars of communications equipment and millions of dollars of safety and backup systems—carries an unusual set of characteristics then that is usually when I might have the interest. And that is likely because I have an interest in select "exotic events."

My initial reaction, if you will, was a necessary foundation for my later analysis, chiefly due to the complexity of the event. I usually write these things down and put them away, but something inside of me, the unknown factor, gave me an indication that the deletion of Flight 370, a tragedy for the families with those onboard and a devastating blow to the nation of Malaysia had another significance—the crux of my argument in the first version of the discussion.

The first version, strangely so, did gain some fleeting interest—I've never had strong interest in any of my books so even a fleeting interest was noted—and I decided to put the smallish book, if you called it that, into a print version. Whether some people preferred printed pages or whether someone was documenting "what not to do as a writer" we may never know. What we do know is that I wasn't afraid to use the "remote flying of the plane" card, which the aviation experts and newsrooms tended to avoid. The printed book also had fleeting interest from the point of view of a self-publisher.

I gathered my notes, collected my thoughts, listened to CNN day-after-day, and before any search operation started, I wrote and published my little book. Having published it, I was content that I had communicated my key messages well, aside from them having the expected depth, and considering the fact that it was early in the mysterious event process. My chosen style was to add the direct references into the body of the discussion, since the book wasn't expected to be very long as an ebook. Again, the lack of references may have scared some "intelligent" people away but everything was included in the body of the text. Plus, I never liked end notes. This edition, in the name of doing things better, includes end notes.

I had always intended to expand my analysis in the future, but needed to have put forth what I knew beforehand. And the reason for me is straightforward, though I realize that in the real world it can come across as outlandish and conspiratorial. I didn't care. My rogue research, which already had dated back to Edward Snowden in 2013, had been building a *different* case, a case having to do with the weaponization of the weather. Hence, the title, *World War C*, with "C" referring to climate and "world" referring to the 4.5 billion year old rock that is floating in space and "war" referring to that thing we do just because we can't figure out what else to do with full metal jackets.

See, I wasn't writing this book because I was some aviation expert, and if anyone thought that then they read the wrong book because I am *not* an aviation expert. I don't consider myself to be a conspiracy theorist. I tend to do my own thing. My own research. I tend to present extremely provocative ideas, and some of them make more sense over time. MH370, it turned out, provided me with an essential piece to my puzzle.

You know how when you are making a puzzle and you have most of the picture but you can't figure out a couple of major pieces because they are too obscure or misleading? That was where I was at with my weather weapons picture puzzle. I had a growing body of evidence that weather bombs had been used to create climate catastrophes, some of which may have stimulated the climatologists into action. I had some inclination as to who were the players, but I wasn't sure—until Mr. Snowden popped his head into the scene.

Ex-CIA Edward Snowden launched onto the scene exposing mass government surveillance and became a refugee after going public. He made his escape and the only country that could shield him from the wrath of his former employers was Russia and the KGB, the enemy of America. That was another piece to my puzzle.

Some more puzzle pieces fit together later in 2013 when the Ukraine experienced a political coup and America was hit with a Thanksgiving winter storm. We later found out that Russia wanted Ukraine back and that confirmed for me that it was Russia who had hit America with a storm.

How is that even possible?

I told you, I deal in exotic events and from my experience with exotic events these are not discussions for everyone, and I know that, and my readers reflect that. But the central theme of *World War C* has to do with climate weapons. Because I have evidence that Russia has them and has been using them on America. All of this is hush-hush top secret. There's almost no way I will get a full public disclosure on the secret climate war that's been going on. Wait a minute; I do have two senior level US Cabinet members stating this is a fact, 18 years apart from one another. And I have some other evidence as well.

Are you seeing a picture yet? Because you should be. And the picture shows that the tensions between President Obama and President Putin had been growing and after the CIA took out the pro-Russian president of the Ukraine that's when Putin sent in the military to Crimea. We all remember Crimea. You can see all the moving parts to this picture puzzle and why it was necessary for me to write a book early.

The puzzle is not only complex, it also spans a number of vastly different fields, from geopolitics to climatology to aviation, many of which I have zero expertise in. Let's be honest. If I had any expertise I wouldn't be researching exotic events.

Pushing forward, Russia was upset about what the CIA and the IMF did to the Ukraine. America was being blasted by a polar vortex at the top of 2014. It was freezing in America thanks to Putin. But he wasn't happy. He wanted his Ukraine back. Ukraine was going through major reforms. Putin was getting less happy. The world was watching the USA and Russia fighting. And you know what happened the last time that the then-Soviet Union went up against the United States—the Cold War.

Ukraine is on fire. It's March 2014. Four months after the coup. Eight months after Snowden arrived in Russia. Then it happened—Malaysia Airlines Flight 370 flew off the face of the earth and has never been seen since March 8. As of this writing, June 25, 2016, no plane, debris, or wreckage has ever been found. There is no trace of Flight 370. Former Prime Minister of Malaysia, Dr. Mahathir, has said publicly that the only two groups—CIA and Boeing— that definitely know what happened to the flight aren't talking. They are not only silent but the media has stopped asking them questions.

I know that most people are focused on the commercial jetliner. I know that. I'm not only focused on the jetliner, as I've described. That is because my picture is far more exotic and also because I think that the disappearance of Flight 370 was an exotic crime. Not the usual sort of crime, as we shall see.

Why did MH370 vanish? Because it was necessary.

Now allow me to elaborate a bit further in the hopes that you will see that Flight 370 is several pieces of an otherwise very large puzzle.

There are some big things happening in the world and this is one of those rare moments where we may be able to capture some of that lightening in a bottle (or a book). What I will tell you is what I know. Some of these fields are well outside of my areas of knowledge. I will use other ways to discuss them. My central theme, again, is the secret climate war between Russia and

America, and possibly other players. And if climatologists take this as another attack on their warped theories of melting glaciers and homeless polar bears then so be it.

If it isn't clear, when you believe in a theory of weather manipulation and climate modification technologies you automatically stop listening to any theory regarding Climate Change simply for the fact that the numbers have been influenced by advanced meteorological technologies.

These three things form the central arguments in this newly revised book—Russia vs. America, climate wars, Flight 370. These three pillars together form the fourth pillar and it has to do with weather weapons.

I don't have all the answers. I do think that the puzzle pieces fit and that the (initial) picture reveals the deployment of classified weapons. If my theory is even mildly accurate, and a climate war is raging between two superpowers, I think the public should have some awareness of that scenario. If this book helps to do that, great.

"MH370 is a Boeing 777 aircraft. It was built and equipped by Boeing. All the communications and GPS equipment must have been installed by Boeing. If they failed or have been disabled Boeing must know how it can be done."

~ DR. MAHATHIR MOHAMAD, FORMER PRIME
MINISTER OF MALAYSIA

"The US reaffirms its commitment to Ukraine's sovereignty. The United States reaffirms its commitment to Ukraine's sovereignty and territorial integrity. According to international law, we condemn the Russian Federation's act of aggression. There is nothing strong in what Russia is doing."
~ JOHN KERRY, U.S. SECRETARY OF
STATE

"Others are engaging even in an eco-type of terrorism whereby they can alter the climate, set off earthquakes, volcanoes remotely through the use of electromagnetic waves."
~ WILLIAM COHEN, US SECRETARY OF DEFENSE,
APRIL 28, 1997

PARIS *TOSEN*

PART 1

Russia vs. America

CHAPTER 1

A COLD WAR BREWS ON THE STOVE OF DEMOCRACY

"Truth is stranger than fiction, but it is because Fiction is obliged to stick to possibilities; Truth isn't." ~ MARK TWAIN

There is a mystery at work here.

2014. At the top of January there was an Arctic storm. By February, there had been a coup d'état in Ukraine and Russia grabbed the Crimean Peninsula. Come March, as we witness the cusp of a real-time Russian invasion into Ukraine, with the United States and other western powers wary of a new Cold War, the strangest thing in the history of aviation happens—a commercial Boeing 777 out of Kuala Lumpur on its way to Beijing disappears.

Into thin air.

Gone.

It gets stranger. June 2013. A 29-year-old American named Edward Snowden, on the run from U.S. authorities, after taking classified documents from the most secure computer ever invented, finds himself in Russia, his passport cancelled and trapped at the airport. Mr. Snowden had just made public an ongoing and unwarranted—what many people saw as illegal and unconstitutional—mass surveillance program by the NSA (National Security Agency). Despite objections from U.S. President Barack Obama, and after more than 20 nations rejected Mr. Snowden's application for asylum, pressured to do so from the U.S., Russia offers him a one-year renewable asylum.

On the surface, aside from Putin and Obama, these seemingly disparate events—Arctic storm, Ukrainian coup, Russia's military, Putin, Obama, Cold War, Malaysia Airlines Flight 370—have very little in common. The weather has nothing in common with the Cold War. Obama has no connection to Malaysia Airlines. Snowden has no friends in Ukraine. *World War C* will argue that these series of strange, even mysterious, events are all intimately connected in ways we've never before imagined. Further, I will argue that the vanishing of Flight 370, as tragic as it is, de-escalated an improvised war between the U.S. and Russia. I will show that this stream of events is related and I will at least partially expose covert and secret technologies being displayed on the geopolitical stage.

These events happened, more or less, in this order: Edward Snowden, Russian asylum, Obama and Putin standoff over Snowden, Arctic storm in the United States, Ukrainian revolution, more Obama and Putin standoff over Ukraine, more Arctic storm, Ukrainian coup d'état, Russia takes Crimean Peninsula, threat of Cold War between United States and Russia, mysterious disappearance of Flight MH370, Republic of Crimea joins Russian Federation, Obama and Putin standoff over Crimea, Flight MH370 vanishes over the Indian Ocean, Cold War warms up.

Russia doesn't invade Ukraine. And if it does, it doesn't lead to war.

It started with Snowden.

Exactly how did ex-NSA contractor Edward Snowden trigger a new Cold War with the United States and Russia? And how come there was no Cold War? Recall that the threat of a Cold War didn't originate from some left or right wing activist or conspiracy theorist, rather it came from the highest levels of political office—John

Kerry, Barack Obama, Hillary Clinton, Mikhail Gorbachev, Mitt Romney.

"Governor Romney, I'm glad that you recognize that Al Qaida is a threat, because a few months ago when you were asked what's the biggest geopolitical threat facing America, you said Russia, not Al Qaida; you said Russia, in the 1980s, they're now calling to ask for their foreign policy back because, you know, the Cold War's been over for 20 years." ~ PRESIDENT OBAMA SAID TO PRESIDENTIAL NOMINEE MITT ROMNEY IN THE THIRD 2012 TELEVISED POLITICAL DEBATES

"Our approach as the United States is not to see these as some Cold War chessboard in which we're in competition with Russia." ~ PRESIDENT OBAMA, FEBRUARY 19, 2014

"We're hoping that Russia will not see this as sort of a continuation of the Cold

War." ~ SECRETARY JOHN KERRY, FEBRUARY 26, 2014

"We're not trying to make this a new Cold War." ~ SECRETARY JOHN KERRY, MARCH 2, 2014

"Our main task is to stop the dangerous escalation and find a solution that would be supported by Ukrainian and Russian citizens and prevent a new Cold War." ~ FORMER SOVIET LEADER MIKHAIL GORBACHEV, MARCH 14, 2014

"I hope there is not another Cold War. Obviously, nobody wants to see that. I think that is primarily up to Putin." ~ FORMER SECRETARY OF STATE HILLARY CLINTON, MARCH 18, 2014

This was real and public chatter. And if the Cold War reality was real, evidenced by Russia's military movement in Crimea and along the Ukrainian border, then what took place that could've warmed up relations between these two superpowers?

What happened was the vanishing of Malaysia Airlines Flight MH370. To get a better sense of these geopolitical chess moves, we need to look at each of these events in more detail. Those details will provide us with a clearer image of what is really going on beneath the surface because that is the essential discussion in this book; that political negotiations are being influenced by not only clandestine activities, but, and more importantly, arrangements between nations—even superpowers—are being antagonized by covert technologies not yet (properly) made public. This book will expose one or two covert antagonizing technologies.

This particular crime is interesting to me not only because it has a mysterious nature but also because the entire disappearance of the plane out of Kuala Lumpur on March 8, 2014 has an exotic signature. Over the last 10 years, I have examined a number of exotic crimes, including 9/11, culminating in my short book *Five Hundred Trillion to One: Odds of Collapsing Three Towers* where I used probability and math to explain the illogic of the events on September 11, 2001; and as well, I have discovered some new crimes, as I highlighted in my 2016 book, *Persons Artificial*. In *Persons*, I provided video evidence and unprecedented analysis regarding the existence of three androids on Capitol Hill. These synthetic humans, specifically, had been activated to push through the 2008 Wall Street Bailout and to convince Americans as to the merits of Obamacare in 2009. The involvement of these artificial people highlighted the manipulative state at the highest levels of political power in the most powerful nation in the world. And all of this was highly controversial.

The process of studying exotic crimes allowed me to develop a new set of observational skills. It also allowed me to see the exotic signature of designed events. The more the mystery of Malaysia Airlines Flight 370 grew, and the less conventional sense it made, the more I began to realize that this was an exotic crime. This book is not based on psychic ability and tea leaves, rather the contents herein are based on a new kind of analysis, rooted in facts and logic, but unorthodox enough so as to explain one of the most mysterious events in aviation history. This is lateral thinking past the point of conspiracy.

There's no doubt that the disappearance of MH370 and the loss of 239 lives onboard is a tragedy and those families will forever remember the loss of their loved ones. By the same token, if I'm right, Flight 370 may have saved many more lives when all things are considered. But was the prevention of death their end goal? Was this an act of altruism? Admittedly, it is early in the process, just 15 months after an exotic crime took place, and we are still short on details and facts and an unfinished search operation. My argument will make assumptions and use the many facts that have been made publicly available, and it will also rely on the hours and hours of daily discussions that were televised on CNN, which ran wall-to-wall coverage of the mystery of Flight 370.

During a period of 15 months, the world has seen an endless assortment of theories on Flight 370—rogue pilot, terrorists, aliens, black hole, shot down, mechanical failure, lithium ion battery explosion in cargo hold, invisible plane, meteor strike, sign of God, aliens, cabin fire, Illuminati, zombie plane—most if not all have been debunked. What remains consistent is the fact that no theory, expert or conspiratorial, adequately explains all the steps that were used to make this plane disappear.

An exotic crime is powerfully deceptive because of its mysterious nature and it is vital that the best ideas are brought forward as early as possible, even if they're wrong. Presenting ideas now will hasten a future resolution and may also provide further context to a difficult situation.

It is my intention to add my theory to the discussion at its earliest opportunity in the hopes that the vanishing plane will one day no longer be a mystery. Because even a conventional explanation, as we saw with 9/11, does not adequately explain an exotic crime. And we don't need a new mystery to hang over our heads.

CHAPTER 2

UKRAINE IN WINTER

*"The US reaffirms its commitment to
Ukraine's sovereignty. The United States
reaffirms its commitment to Ukraine's
sovereignty and territorial integrity.
According to international law, we
condemn the Russian Federation's act of
aggression. There is nothing strong in
what Russia is doing."* ~ JOHN KERRY,
U.S. SECRETARY OF STATE

The disappearance of Flight 370 happens to take
place during a tense time between Russia and the
U.S. I'm watching CNN, its 8:05 a.m. on March
20 President Obama is walking to make a speech
on Ukraine. He is updating America's response to
the illegitimate stance of the Russians in the
Crimean Peninsula. The United States has

decided to further punish the Russian government with additional sanctions, while Russian military forces assemble around Ukraine.

Obama is concerned about Russia's escalation in the region and the need to stabilize Ukraine's economy. IMF (International Monetary Fund) is providing additional support to the Ukrainian government. He emphasizes that Russia and the U.S. still have diplomatic ties and that Russia must recognize Ukraine's sovereignty. The speech is held at the White House on his way to board Marine One, the presidential helicopter. It lasted no more than four minutes by my count.

The Ukrainian crisis, ending in the annexation of Crimea, is continuing to heat up. The U.S. Administration has continued to impose sanctions on Russian leaders and their co-conspirators. Obama noted in the speech that he has signed an Executive Order to further ramp up those financial disincentives.

Ukraine shares a long history with communist Russia, only becoming independent in 1990 with Ukrainian law firmly in place and then in August 1991, following the attempted coup in the Soviet Union, which failed to remove Mikhail Gorbachev, the Ukraine declared itself a democratic state. What followed in the 1990s was severe economic recession and civil unrest. By

2000, the economy began to grow amid a young and unstable government.

In 2010, after a handful of corrupt leaders, the pro-Moscow Viktor Yanukovych was elected president. But Mr. Yanukovych didn't want to cooperate with the European Union and starting in November 2013 the mass protests and civil unrest started. Months of deadly riots and protests ensued, and on February 22, 2014 the Members of the Ukraine Parliament decided to impeach the president. The vote failed with less than the required 75% majority.

"First, the issue legitimacy. As you may know, we have a direct appeal from the incumbent and, as I said, legitimate President of Ukraine, Mr Yanukovych, asking us to use the Armed Forces to protect the lives, freedom and health of the citizens of Ukraine." ~ VLADIMIR PUTIN, PRESIDENT OF RUSSIA

The Russian President Vladimir Putin declared the impeachment illegal, citing international interference, and on February 26, 2014 took control of the Crimean Peninsula, an autonomous republic (province) once belonging to the Soviet Union, but now associated with Ukraine. On

March 6, 2014, the Crimean Parliament decided to join the Russian Federation and set a date for a referendum, which included the question:

Do you support rejoining Crimea with Russia as a subject of the Russian Federation?

Then following an interim government in the Ukraine, the Crimean Parliament declared independence on March 11, 2014. The referendum followed and an overwhelming majority voted for the Republic of Crimea to join the Russian Federation. And agreement was signed on **March 18, 2014**.

U.S. Secretary of State John Kerry stated that Washington saw the referendum as illegal and wouldn't recognize it, and neither would the international community, threatening sanctions against Russia. The struggle for Ukraine, to join the European Union or Russia, has ignited a new Cold War between America and Russia. The International Monetary Fund (IMF) had been working with Kiev to rebuild their economic and financial policies.

ARCTIC STORM

The civil unrest in Ukraine coincided with anomalous weather activity in the United States and parts of Canada. In November 2013, right next to Thanksgiving week, a deadly winter storm struck the U.S. The Arctic blast of ice and snow caused flight delays and cancellations, power outages, school and business closures, and dangerous driving conditions. Then in January 2014, the unprecedented winter records and temperature anomalies, dubbed "polar vortex," led to further weather deviations impacting over 200 million people.

Stratospheric shifts led to further weather deviations and lower temperatures due to bitter wind. Many cities recorded an unusually cold February. The State of Iowa, for example, recorded the coldest winter since the late 70s. Eastern Canada was also hit with temperature records. Record lows, coldest winters, heavy snowfall, bitter winds, power outages—these all continued into March 2014.

Weather experts noted that this was significant weather event and some scientists were suggesting that this extreme weather was due to climate change, an accelerated melting of polar ice caps. Winter and Russia culminated in the

2014 Winter Olympics held in Sochi, Russia from February 7-23. It was also significant because it was the first Olympics to be held in Russia since 1991, the year the Soviet Empire collapsed.

You can imagine the significance of the dates of the events *so far*:

2013
June—Edward Snowden blows the whistle on the NSA, he lands in Russia with no passport

August—Snowden granted asylum in Russia

November—Ukraine riots, Arctic blast in America

2014
January—Polar Vortex hits America, everything freezes, civil unrest in Ukraine

February—Ukraine president ousted, Russia occupies Crimea, Winter Olympics in Sochi, occupation of Crimea, more freezing in America

March—Crimea joins Russia, America and Russia on the verge of war, Malaysia Flight 370 vanishes, Russia expelled from G7

EDWARD SNOWDEN

In May 2013, while stationed in Hawaii and earning $122,000 a year, ex-CIA and former NSA contractor Edward Snowden released a host of classified documents to a number of media outlets. Branded both a hero and a traitor, Snowden's desire "to inform the public" turned him into a fugitive among American authorities. He escaped to Hong Kong. En route to Russia his passport was cancelled and his plan to reach Ecuador was thwarted. He still lives in Russia.

Those leaked documents began to be published on June 5, 2013, and continued in the months to follow. The fallout in the Obama administration was measurable and Obama lost favoritism among his people, this was followed by repeated denials and tricky explanations, citing Snowden's actions as treasonous and his claims unsubstantiated. The details of a global and domestic surveillance apparatus between the NSA and its four partners (Canada, United Kingdom, New Zealand, Australia), the "Five Eyes," that routinely scanned civilian phone calls, emails, and, as well, spied on world leaders, such as Germany's Chancellor Angela Merkel, an ally of the U.S. Threats to public privacy became a major concern. Was the government breaking privacy laws?

The NSA scandal also multiplied political tensions between the U.S. and everyone else. Director of National Intelligence, James Clapper, denied these surveillance programs to Congress citing metadata as legal data, and later was identified as lying while under oath. President Obama went public on August 7, 2013, and on *The Tonight Show* told host Jay Leno, "There is no spying on Americans. We don't have a domestic spying program." He wanted to reassure Americans that their privacy was not an issue and to counter Snowden's revelations. The stolen NSA documents would prove to be far more convincing in the months that followed.

Snowden's arrival at Moscow's Sheremetyevo Airport on June 23, 2013 was meant as a transfer point before heading out to Ecuador. But now without a passport, he was forced to stay. On August 1, 2013 he was granted asylum by the Russian government. He had applied to 20 countries asylum but pressures from the U.S. Administration made sure that those requests were rejected. As his applications were routinely not considered, he applied for temporary asylum in Russia. Once again the U.S. Administration pressured Putin not to accept the application and to return him to the United States to face justice. Putin stepped aside and talks continued between mutual federal agencies.

In March 2014, the European Union said that it will suspend the G8 meetings planned for June in Sochi, and that additional sanctions will be handed out to Russia because of its annexation of the Crimean Peninsula. Russia joined the G-7 (Italy, Japan, Germany, Canada, France, United Kingdom, United States) in 1998. On March 24, Russia was expelled from the G7 countries and a meeting was held in Brussels, Belgium on June 4, 2014, without Russia.

There's the government change in Ukraine happening alongside Snowden's asylum in Russia. Obama might've been thinking he would get Snowden back and reassures the American people. Putin steps aside. Snowden stays. Then they take out Ukraine. America gets hit with a fierce winter blast from November through till March. During that time, lots of things afoot.

GOODBYE KIEV

March 7, the Crimean Parliament decided to join Russia. March 8, Malaysia Airlines Flight 370 disappeared into thin air. In February, the

Ukrainian President was deposed and the IMF was instructed to rebuild Kiev's financial policy. In January, the United States experienced the Polar Vortex. In November 2013, Ukraine's revolution began. Simultaneously in November 2013, a freak Arctic storm ravaged the U.S. Back in August 2013, Snowden was given asylum in Russia, a move that angered the United States and stiffened relations with the Kremlin.

Is the U.S. and Russia on the verge of a Cold War or is this being manufactured for other reasons?

The loss of Ukraine under Yanukovych happened in a matter of months. In just a few months, anti-government protestors grabbed a hold of Independence Square through a violent and chaotic uprising. Explosions, smoke, and fire plagued Kiev until what remained of a pro-Moscow leadership, sharply criticized by Obama, was effectively decapitated in what Putin himself regarded as a western-influenced coup d'état.

The veracity and speed of the Ukrainian collapse worked to dissolve Yanukovych's political power base. With a series of political resignations, the President of Ukraine became a target for impeachment. But the coup also had the hallmarks of what ex-NSA employee and former economic hit man, John Perkins, calls the "jackals."

Perkins, author of *Confessions of an Economic Hitman* (2004), worked in the 1980s to assist in the overthrow of governments with only a little bloodshed and no military intervention using instruments such as the World Bank and the IMF. Perkins cites the assassinations of the leader of Ecuador and Panama, Jaime Roldós Aguilera and Omar Torrijos, respectively. But he explains the use of jackals, essentially CIA assassination squads, who would go into a country and attempt to overthrow the government, *coup d'état*, and failing that the leaders would be assassinated. Should all those attempts fail, as Perkins notes was the case with Saddam Hussein, the leader of Iraq—mostly because of his many doubles—then the last option was military invasion. Iraq was invaded in 2003 in a coalition led by the U.S. and the United Kingdom. He was captured on December 13, 2003 and executed three years later.

Why would the United States want to take out the Ukrainian leader? Was it because he was friendly to the Kremlin? Or was there something else going on? In fact, is it possible that taking out Ukraine was an economic hit on Russia? Because Ukraine is an important corridor for Russian natural gas to the European Union, Moscow and Kiev ran into a standoff in 2006 after Ukraine couldn't pay off its gas debts with Russia. According to the BBC, Ukraine is responsible for 80% of the gas destined for the EU. Control of Ukraine by a pro-EU leader could create heighten gas tensions with Russia which exported four times the U.S. supply abroad. With control of Ukraine, the U.S. natural gas industry might find additional buyers and Russia could be hurt economically, essentially an economic attack. Whatever the reason may be, something caused Putin to take over the Crimean Peninsula and he might still want Ukraine back.

At the same time that the civil unrest started in Kiev, the continental United States was hit with an unusually severe Arctic cold front.

PART 2
Climate Wars

CHAPTER 3

THE MAKINGS OF WORLD WAR C

"Why was it necessary to drop the nuclear bomb if LeMay was burning up Japan? And he went on from Tokyo to firebomb other cities. 58% of Yokohama. Yokohama is roughly the size of Cleveland. 58% of Cleveland destroyed. Tokyo is roughly the size of New York. 51% percent of New York destroyed. 99% of the equivalent of Chattanooga, which was Toyama. 40% of the equivalent of Los Angeles, which was Nagoya. This was all done before the dropping of the nuclear bomb, which by the way was dropped by LeMay's command. Proportionality should be a guideline in war. Killing 50% to 90% of the people of 67 Japanese cities and then bombing them with two nuclear bombs is not proportional, in the minds of some people, to the objectives we were trying to achieve." ~ ROBERT S. MCNAMARA, FORMER US SECRETARY OF DEFENSE, "The Fog of War"

On April 28, 1997 when U.S. Secretary of Defense William Cohen said in response to a question at a DoD News Briefing: "Others are engaging even in an eco-type of terrorism whereby they can alter the climate, set off earthquakes, volcanoes remotely through the use of electromagnetic waves," only the conspiracy theorists understood the existence of Climate Weapons—and that some agency is using them against America. That's no longer a theory. Fast-forward to 2014 and this time Secretary of State John Kerry makes this amazing statement during a speech on February 17, 2014, "In a sense, climate change can now be considered the world's largest weapon of mass destruction, perhaps even, the world's most fearsome weapon of mass destruction."

The head of the Pentagon, a top Cabinet member, is regularly briefed on all matters of national security, including all levels of threats. Most of this information is classified and subject to treason; therefore, when Kerry, also top Cabinet member, equates climate change on the order of "weapons of mass destruction" we should take special note.

Climate weapons have always belonged in science fiction movies, and the fictional genre, because it was understood that we didn't have these technologies that could create snow storms, hurricanes, tornadoes, and earthquakes. We took our weather at face value and blamed it on Mother Nature. Whether it was the Category 5 Hurricane Andrew in 1992, Hurricane Katrina in 2005 over the Gulf Coast, or, more recently, Hurricane Sandy in 2012 over New York City. The economic costs are in the tens of billions of dollars.

In a 1976 episode from the popular TV series, *The Bionic Woman*, a former scientist of OSI (Office of Science Intelligence) steals a top secret weather-control machine in order to terrorize the world. Jaime Sommers, the bionic woman, is joined by Col. Steve Austin, the six million dollar man, to stop the evil scientist and they must face manufactured storms and a slew of *fembots*, female androids. That was 40 years ago.

The idea that there is a device that can generate unique weather patterns is not as far-fetched as the mainstream would have you believe. In fact, the truth is far more severe and perplexing and it has virtually nothing to do with Climate Change, brainchild of Al Gore and propagated through his 2006 documentary, *An Inconvenient Truth*. While former Vice President of the United States Gore insists the dire emergency of climate change, according to activist Naomi Klein, the Science Advisory Committee of Lyndon B.

Johnson's administration warned about climate change in 1965. The climate threat had been around for over 40 years, without any governmental push; not even during the 8-year Clinton administration.

The weather-making machines of the science fiction genre have been in use for some time. The following "weather anomalies" were a result of weather control machines. There will be many in the alternative camp who will point to HAARP (High Frequency Active Auroral Research Program), a DARPA-related program that tests ionospheric influence using high frequency bandwidths directed at the ionosphere. HAARP is frequently cited by conspiracy theorists as the reason for unusual natural disasters, for example, when 100,000 fish were found dead in the Arkansas River in 2011 and only one species of fish, drum fish, had died. This followed the inexplicable death of thousands of birds. I'm not a HAARP enthusiast because I like to think there are other weapons hiding in our orbit.

One victim of the so-called "unexpected weather" and large amounts of rainfall was in the Canadian province of Alberta. On June 20, 2013 the City of Calgary had record rainfall of 45 millimeters in one day, up to 200 millimeters of rainfall in some areas. Canmore, a small town 81 kilometers west of Calgary, saw more rainfall in 6 hours than in 6 months.

As cited by one resident, Cougar Creek, normally 10-feet wide and 6-inches deep grew to 30-meters wide and 10-meters deep because of the torrential downpours. The Albertan floods became a national emergency. The TransCanada Highway, all four lanes of it, was under water, Calgary was severely flooded, and 175,000 Albertans were under evacuation orders. The National Guard had to be bee deployed.

When did Glenn Greenwald and Edward Snowden release the NSA documents? It started on June 5, 2013. When did Snowden land in Russia? June 23. Is it coincidental that Calgary gets flooded at the same time? But the Calgary flood didn't originate in Canada. It originated in the United States.

Overall, more rain fell in 60 hours than in 30 days. Meteorologists reasoned that the Albertan storm started in Denver, Colorado on June 18 at 2:24 pm, moving up through Utah at phenomenal speed and the high pressure system then became trapped over the region.

Natural disasters, because of the theory of climate change, have increasingly been either enhanced by global warming or explained by it. Just in the beginning of 2014, an Arctic cold front, dubbed "Polar Vortex," hit the Midwestern and eastern United States, and parts of Canada. The heavy snowfall and extreme low temperatures affected 200 million people, even breaking the cold-weather records going back 30 or 40 years.

But climate weapons can do a lot more than just stir up the eye of a storm as it did the one that hit New Orleans. They can also create earthquakes by beaming electromagnetic waves into the planet's tectonic plates. And the results could include the Haiti earthquake in 2010 where 200,000 people died. These electromagnetic weapons are adding a new paradigm in the geopolitical divide. There was also the Japan earthquake in 2011. The last time an earthquake of that magnitude hit was 1,200 years ago and it was the fifth most powerful earthquake in the world. The Earth shifted its axis by nearly one foot. Is it Mother Nature, ie climate change due to fossil fuels, or is it Eco-Terrorism hiding behind the mask of climate change?

The Secretary of State, sworn to the highest levels of secrecy and briefed by all security agencies, can't very well tell Americans that its enemies have deployed electromagnetic weapons against their nation and this has been the reason behind weather catastrophes. Because we've seen a lot of weather anomalies since the 1990s. First of all, it would be an act of treason to betray national secrets.

By the same token, the obviousness of the attacks has become (almost) unavoidable and Kerry had no choice but to make a veiled statement. In an age where nuclear attacks are prohibited and frowned upon by the world, what better way to decimate your enemy than by a weather bomb just as powerful and with less radioactive fallout, and with no fingerprints?

Now it's our step, isn't it? At least two high-level US officials, spanning 17 years, have identified "eco-terrorism" whereby agents in charge of back-engineered climate weapons are torturing Americans, economically and psychologically, in order to squeeze the U.S. Administration, under President Obama, into offering better terms in secret negotiations. And we have to at least imply that there are secret negotiations going on about the geopolitical divide.

CHAPTER 4

THE WEATHER BOMB

We take the weather for granted. We are at the mercy of the weather. We make clothing to protect us against all kinds of weather conditions. In doing so, we have admitted that the weather cannot be conquered. Our obeisance to the weather is so natural for us that after millennia of human evolution, in every nation around the world, we have acquiesced to the power of nature. We no longer question Mother Nature because she has proven to be more powerful than our entire species.

  The weather is not God. We don't worship the weather. Neither is the weather the Devil. The weather is a stranger. The weather is unpredictable and powerful. A hurricane can take out an entire city such as we saw when Hurricane Katrina hit New Orleans. An earthquake can devastate a nation. We saw this when Haiti earthquake struck in 2010. Or a tsunami the result of a massive underwater earthquake, one powerful tsunami on December 26, 2004 and 200,000 lives were lost.

Then again, the weather is as powerful as God. With one earthquake hundreds of thousands of lives can be taken out. No divine wrath. Sins and sinners killed equally. A hurricane can destroy a city's infrastructure. We recognize the power of earthquakes and natural disasters. Seismologists know that an earthquake releases a tremendous amount of energy.

Little Boy, the bomb dropped on Hiroshima contained 140-pounds of uranium-235 and created a blast of 15 kilotons (the equivalent of 15,000 tons of TNT, trinitrotoluene). The Nagasaki bomb, *Fat Man*, with 14-pounds of plutonium delivered a 21 kiloton blast. Combined together, that amounts to 36 kilotons.

An 8.6 magnitude earthquake releases the equivalent of a 230 megaton thermonuclear weapon. The Russians detonated a 50 megaton bomb in 1961, the largest ever recorded. It weighed 60,000 pounds and was 26-feet long. The volcanic eruption of Krakatoa in 1883 is said to have had a yield of 200 megatons.

Think of the 2004 Indonesian earthquake, measured out at 9.0 magnitude, would have had a yield of 475 megatons (millions of tons of TNT).

The chief difference between an atomic bomb and a weather bomb (or, earthquake) is accountability. We have restrictions on the deployment of atomic weapons, Nuclear Non-Proliferation Treaty for example, we don't have restrictions on natural disasters, that is, no party, agency, nation or group can be held accountable. What happens if we could create earthquakes and volcanic eruptions? Or we could generate tornadoes and hurricanes? My argument includes evidence that at least two nations have developed climate-based weapons, namely America and Russia—and a good number of recent "natural disasters" were a result of a weather bomb.

There's no traditional way to determine whether an earthquake is real or artificial. When you study an earthquake, or a hurricane, you study the damage; you study the meteorological patterns so that you can predict another storm. The better your prediction the more likely lives will be saved. A hurricane and an earthquake are two very different natural disasters. One has to do with weather and wind patterns, the other with geophysical plate movements.

How do we know if a natural event is artificial? You have to study motive. You need to understand the geopolitical divide. Why did the USA drop two atomic bombs on Japan? Because the Empire of Japan was threatening the peace and stability of the world order. Geopolitics. There was a real motive to end World War II. What would Russia have against Haiti? Why did Hurricane Sandy strike the eastern US border?

Besides natural disasters, we have storms. Storms are less destructive but also crippling. Fewer deaths but still effective. Winter storms slow things down. Unusual droughts can cripple an area of water. A grape growing region without water could seriously alter the wine market.

We've already looked at a number of storms; I'd like to focus on a selection of earthquakes. This is a selection that has the hallmark of modification and amplification. Earthquakes love a heavy body count, and it is often the case that humans who need to make statements need to show lots of body bags. Nature isn't interested in mass murder. In fact, natural earthquakes are the result of shifts in tectonic plates, or the release of stored energy and the Earth tends to find, but not always, places that are not heavily populated.

We could also say that our civilization has urbanized areas that have, historically and scientifically, proven not to be in a distressed area. If you're going to build a city, or a 100-storey office building, you're going to consult with geologists and seismologists. They're going to show data on your real estate. The development of an urban area has been studied vigorously. We can say that the large cities of today have been built on areas that are not prone to ecological disasters; therefore, when a city is struck and the body bags run out of stock there's usually a human involved.

The challenge for me is to show you without any whistleblower or first-hand evidence. The other challenge is to convince you, at least somewhat, that a good selection of ecological disasters has been artificially-induced and those humans have a lot of blood on their hands. We're going to have to redefine the term "mass murderer."

If there are nations and groups with regular access to weapons that can effectively yield up to 475 megatons per deployment, then we need to establish a new kind of anti-proliferation treaty. We've done away with atomic warfare because the human cost is too high and the damage to our environment is too grim. We've avoided a nuclear winter.

In its place, well-funded mad scientists have engineered the polar vortex and the earthquake-generated tsunami. Nations have stockpiled thousands of nuclear weapons just in case the arrival of a doomsday. Society has remained under the threat of atomic war and the end of mankind. While all that was going on, other men, the kind that believe they rule the world, have developed advanced climate-class weaponry. They've tested this weaponry. They've deployed these devices. And no one even blinked an eye. No one blinked an eye because no one ever thought if that earthquake was artificial.

The death toll from climate weapons and atomic weapons is very similar. The economic damage is similar. Destruction of the infrastructure, if you've ever seen images of a city that has been struck by an earthquake, is similar. Climate weapons excel in that they leave no fingerprints and they lack radioactive fallout, verily climate weapons are the new bombs.

CHAPTER 5

ELECTROMAGNETIC SUPERHEATERS

It is hard to imagine that some agency would cause an earthquake to rupture leading to the death of thousands of people. I agree. It is hard to imagine. Similarly, it is hard to imagine that a 21 kiloton bomb would be dropped on a heavily populated area. It is also hard to imagine that a country would invade another country and kill children. Even harder to imagine that a powerful nation would capture innocent civilians, take them to a camp and to ritualistically kill them solely based on their race. Do you still find it hard to imagine some agency causing an earthquake?

Now think about the leaders of these nations that have in their possession climate weapons, why there are treaties to prevent nuclear armament and detonation but there are no visible treaties against earthquake weapons. Suppose that a group of four earthquakes since 2004, killing one million people, turned out had been artificially-induced. Should those people be held accountable? Do societies have the right to know about these ultra-advanced technologies? Because the people who are dying are not soldiers. The people are civilians. Pretty much all civilians. They're dead because of a secret geopolitical divide. Civilians are given no warning, no notice, no preparation, no particular help with the trauma and no one is ever held accountable.

Had Russia hit New Orleans with a tactical nuclear strike, what would've happened? An attack in Russia, likely the start of WWIII. Also likely, a terrible time for humanity.

Let's be honest, the people in charge are thinking that secrecy is better than an all-out war. They're also thinking that a hurricane bomb is better than an atomic bomb. Sure, an earthquake is powerful but those happen outside the U.S. boundary. Major earthquake strikes on American soil don't happen. They do happen to American allies and enemies.

Should I be correct in my alternative hypothesis that there is a Climate War between Russia and the United States then it would be important to expose these clandestine technologies and to be aware of future catastrophic events. We are at a time in human history where our need to know is being superseded by "our right" to know.

For me, it started in 2010. It was January. I was living in Kelowna, British Columbia. I had a full time job as a night janitor and in my spare time I was prognosticating on things that most people were afraid to discuss. I had written and self-published a number of books and was speaking on issues concerning interstellar cultures. On January 12 a magnitude 7.0 earthquake struck outside of Haiti's capital, Port-au-Prince. A death toll nearing 200,000 along with the destruction of infrastructure followed. Millions of people displaced.

True, the fault zone was overdue for an earthquake. But it didn't need any help. It had been more than 200 years since a major earthquake struck Haiti. Former presidents Bill Clinton and George W. Bush got together with President Obama to raise funds to help Haiti. Secretary Hillary Clinton visited the ruins and promised funding for the recovery. Several billion dollars of political support and international recovery teams came to aid the distressed nation, later the recovery effort had fallen apart and progress slowed.

On January 13, 2010, during a live broadcast of CNN's *The Situation Room with Wolf Blitzer*, correspondent Tom Foreman showed Wolf a digital map of the earthquake's strike zone, put together by the US Geological Survey (USGS). Although easier to see on television, Foreman's transcript highlights a very interesting theme:

> So if we move in a little bit closer here, again, and I turn on a different map here, you can take a look at what we call the shake map. The shake map will show you the—sort of the intensity of those areas. So the main hit was here. But you see that much of the shaking has now occurred out this way, not this way. The red area is what we're talking about. Most of its been this way.
>
> If I turn that one off and turn on the actual incidence of tremors—the tremors since the original one, you can see, the original one hit over here. Since then, most of them have been smaller and they've been spread this way. And look at this little red one right here. That red one means that it happened within the past hour. So they're still getting hit, but it's away from the prime area. All of that is good.

Notice how Foreman uses his words "this way" and "over here" and "away from the prime area."

He's describing the direction of the tremors (aftershocks), large ones like "5.6s and 5.9s," according to CNN Meteorologist Chad Meyers. Three days later and Haiti had experienced 35 aftershocks. More importantly, Foreman is describing the fact that the direction of the kinetic energy of an aftershock had changed. He said "much of the shaking has now occurred out this way, not this way." The tremors have turned away from the populated areas. That discussion is more complicated, but it *could* indicate the deployment of a "counter-weapon," something that deflected the kinetic energy shooting up through the earth from the original attack. Did I really say attack?

A terrible thing happened to Haiti in 2010. What if the Haiti earthquake was the result of a climate weapon? What kind of climate weapon could cause tectonic plates to rupture? Electromagnetic superheaters. A particle-beam weapon. Directed energy emitter. Take your pick. Develop a machine to beam charged particles at the speed of light into a target. Make it industrial size. Put one in Earth's orbit without a press release and you have an invisible weapon. It's not complicated.

A directed energy weapon beams kinetic energy into matter. The highly charged particles superheat the target causing it to expand, weaken or even crack. Send enough kinetic energy into an unstable tectonic planet, and what happens? The plate shifts. What happens when the plates of rock under the surface shift? Earthquakes.

You were probably thinking that there as a device that delivers a ready-made earthquake to a given area, kind of like a pizza delivery. When you're dealing with advanced weaponry you have to think out of the conventional warfare box. This is not a 10,000-pound bomb you drop and detonate. This is a particle accelerator shooting out such a tremendous amount of energy into the earth that it causes a shift in the tectonic plates. It would make sense that you use a device on areas noted for their seismological activity. In other words, you won't create an earthquake on a sheet of solid rock.

For a very simplified analogy, think of a microwave oven. Put a raw chicken leg in your oven and watch it cook. You can't see the flames. You can't see the microwaves with your eyes. And the oven is shielded to prevent any leakage. You can put a cup of water in the microwave and you can heat it to the point of boiling. Still, you will not see any microwaves. Imagine that technology on an in industrial scale.

Six weeks after the Haiti earthquake, there's another earthquake near central Chile. On February 27, 2010, Chile is hit with an 8.8, among

the largest earthquakes ever recorded. What did
we say about the yield of an earthquake? We said
that an 8.6 magnitude was equivalent to the yield
of a 230 Mt thermonuclear weapon. At magnitude
8.8, we're pretty much dealing with a huge
amount of energy off the coast of Chile. Five
hundred people died and most of Chile
experienced a power outage lasting several days.
Where did the earthquake originate? Between
major tectonic plates. The plate movement
shifted cities and land mass. It apparently even
moved Buenos Aires an inch west.

   The March 11, 2011 earthquake off the coast of
Japan claimed nearly 20,000 lives. Destruction to
the infrastructure, closing down of major ports,
millions of people without electricity, and even
damage to nuclear reactors. The reactors at
Fukushima were badly damaged after the 9.0
magnitude earthquake struck; enough
radioactivity to cordon off a 30-km zone. The
reactors, partially funded and designed by
General Electric, went into meltdown. This was
Japan's Chernobyl. The 2011 Tohoku
earthquake's epicentre was 70 km off the coast of
Japan. It was so powerful that it moved the island
of Japan 8 feet. Over one million buildings had
either collapsed completely or were badly

damaged, a crisis for the nation unlike anything since Hiroshima and Nagasaki.

Does a climate war need a formal declaration in order for it to be active? Or can we just count the body bags?

CHAPTER 6

THE ARTIFICIAL EARTHQUAKE

We're starting to see a picture of the devastating effects of natural disasters, a type of event that has always been considered to be natural and what I'm arguing is that some of these "natural" events are not natural. As you can see, the challenge is not only identifying good candidates as artificial strikes by a clandestine enemy, but also for the average person to think that there's a new kind of weapon against humanity and there's at least some evidence of deployment. The earthquakes I've pointed out are what I believe to be good candidates for the result of a climate weapon. Obviously, I don't have the technology or the connections to show the data and if these had been atomic detonations we'd all be in a lot of trouble. But these are attacks with few fingerprints and these are weapons that don't officially exist.

What I'm *not* saying is that every earthquake is artificial. That is not my argument. I'm saying that mixed in with natural catastrophes there are artificial catastrophes. And they happen for a reason. We don't know all the reasons. How can we?

It is important to understand that an earthquake is as good, if not better, as a weapon, as is a nuclear warhead. It's better because it's not considered an "act of war" because in order for it to be classified as an act of war these advanced technologies—electromagnetic superheaters— need to be declassified. The declassification of such a weapon would only send the scientific community into a frenzy because they'd want to study particle beam accelerators up close.

Additionally, the release of climate weapons into the public domain would force other advanced technologies into civilian space. We might find other things such as suppressed non-fossil fuel engines or anti-gravitic propulsion systems; perhaps even a homegrown flying saucer and designs for a Martian terraforming platform. You can see why these climate weapons will not be so carelessly revealed. I'm revealing them now as a kind of obligatory gift to humankind with as much substantiation as I can muster with few resources. The reactions will be mostly negative and mixed, in the near future. In the distant future, the reactions will be revised and people might find my wild speculation quite basic.

Moving on, we look back seven years from the Japanese Chernobyl and we visit Indonesia. On Boxing Day, the India and Burma plates danced. It was an undersea strike so severe that it unleashed a tsunami up to 100 feet high. Our planet shook for nearly 10 minutes. By the time it was all done a quarter of a million lives had been lost. Indonesia was the worst hit. Thailand, Sri Lanka and India were also hit. The megathrust earthquake in the Indian Ocean was one of the worst in history. The other megathrusters we've already noted: 2010 Chile earthquake and 2011 Tohoku earthquake. Megathrust earthquakes happen where the most destructive plate boundary conditions exist. My selections took place within a space of about 7 years.

An earthquake is one particular type of artificial catastrophe, one which releases such an immense amount of energy that they can tilt the planet of the Earth. Not an easy thing to do. The term "artificial" is temporary and it has to do with having a man-made architecture. We have the technology to engineer earthquakes and the shift in tectonic plates can ruin nations and take hundreds of thousands of lives without any warning whatsoever.

CHAPTER 7

RUSSIAN EARTHQUAKE RECIPE

The ability to engineer an earthquake is still not publicly known. The ability to decide which disaster is natural and which is engineered is going to be a discussion to be held in the future. Does a small earthquake qualify as an engineered earthquake? Would a nation use a small earthquake as an attack? Because until now we've only been discussing megathrusters and large-scale events.

On Friday, March 28, 2014, President Putin called President Obama at the Ritz Carlton Hotel in Saudi Arabia. Obama was interested in de-escalation in the Ukraine while Putin wanted to voice his concern over the rampage of extremists. Just politics, right? Not exactly. On March 17, a 4.4 magnitude earthquake hit Los Angeles. A 5.1 magnitude quake struck Orange County on March

28, preceded by a 3.6 tremor. This was the second earthquake in two weeks.

On March 1, Obama called Putin who said that he need to do what was necessary. The 90-minute conversation was about Ukraine and Russia's unnecessary military intervention. Putin defended his position and said that Ukrainian extremists were interfering with the pro-US government that had been installed. The standoffs over Ukraine made Putin dig his military heels deeper into the Crimean ground. That night Canada pulled its ambassador from Russia.

At the end of February, after Yanukovych was ousted from Kiev, an interim leader was put in place. The speaking of Russian is going to be banned. By February 28, Russian forces have seized parts of Crimea. March 1, Putin is given approval to use military force in Ukraine. This prompts the 90-minute phone call from Obama.

While Crimea is under the gun and the Ukrainian tensions are rising, far off in Southeast Asia a Boeing 777 on its way to Beijing from Kuala Lumpur disappears off the tip of Sumatra. The vanishing of Flight 370 took place on March 8, smack in the middle of the US and Russia tensions. Suddenly, there's another discussion and it has absolutely nothing to do with a brewing

Cold War, and it has everything to do with Malaysia and 239 people onboard a commercial jetliner. Two weeks into the disappearance of the plane was when I published the first version of this book, *Why Malaysia Airlines Flight 370 Vanished.*

On March 17, the same day an earthquake hits Los Angeles, the EU and US target Russian and Ukrainian officials, freezing their assets and restricting their travel. Coincidence? Perhaps. There's tension between Obama and Putin. Much of this we may not know publicly. March 17 Los Angeles takes a hit by a minor earthquake on the same day that Russian and Ukrainian officials are harassed. We have that, but that isn't enough to make a statement.

Push forward to March 28, now it is a week after my ebook has come out, and Orange County, the third most populated county in California, gets hits with a 3.6 tremor followed an hour later by a 5.1 quake. On March 27, a 2.6 quake hit Huntington Beach. President Obama, in Saudi Arabia, agrees to take a call from President Putin. Three quakes directly *timed* to Russian and American negotiations and geopolitical concerns—unless Mother Nature is Russian it would be virtually impossible for these earthquakes to be so perfectly timed. Not only that but Los Angeles isn't a hotbed for earthquakes. It took three quakes to get Obama to take a phone call from Putin. Can you see the link here between engineered earthquakes and geopolitical tensions?

The timing seems rather impeccable. Was the Earth responding so that the US and Russia could remain friends? Although it is speculative, when you add these smaller events with the rest of the story you get to see the larger puzzle. The puzzle includes a technology that can "dial and deliver" ecological damage. The technology can literally shake the entire Earth as we saw in the 2004 Indonesian undersea quake or the technology can act as a motivational tool to spur two leaders to pick up the phone. Imagine how precise this technology must be for it to have such a range in its dial. This device can dial the magnitude of an earthquake at a precise location, but it must be located on seismological zones, and deliver an outcome that can have a lasting economic impact.

All of these effects are virtually invisible, aside from some of my highlights, and publicly unavailable. They are unavailable to the public because these are ultra-advanced weapons; besides they are great tools for diplomatic resolutions. We can only imagine how often they've been used to sway a political process or to

bring certain concessions to a table of
negotiations. Plus, we don't know, not yet, when
they were invented and who invented them. That
is to say, we don't know how long they've been
using them; and following that train of thought,
we don't know the total body count and economic
impact.

An advanced weapon of ecological destruction is
a weapon of only the most powerful nations. In
this case, I cite Russia and America as two of the
best candidates. On top of these two, I might add
at least one more device in the market, this one
not in the hands of a nation. If rogue groups exist
in every industry then you can bet that a rogue
group, even a coalition of some sort, may have
even an improvised device in their possession, or
with some access to such a device. Had they not a
climate weapon, it would be them writing this
book to expose clandestine super-devices in the
hands of men who refuse to speak the
climatological truth.

CHAPTER 8

RISE OF THE CLIMATE TERRORIST

While "we" don't know "who" is zapping America, we can assume it's not a mad scientist with bad hair and an awful accident. And we assume that Obama knows. But we have a pretty good guess, don't we? American's biggest detractors are Russia, Iran, and North Korea. Considering that Syria is in turmoil and Russia and Iran have an interest here, we might infer that the Polar Vortex was sent as a rebuttal. And Syria has played a pivotal role in all of this. "And this is why, after careful deliberation, I determined that it is in the national security interests of the United States to respond to the Assad regime's use of chemical weapons through a targeted military strike," said Obama in a 2013 speech.

Before climate weapons, the threats were terrorist attacks and nuclear missiles. We were all

sold on "contemporary" and "global" threats.
Homeland security has locked down America
under these pretenses. But the most deaths and
economic damage have come via eco-terrorists
who don't officially exist and who have learned to
weaponize weather.

We should listen to Kerry and read between the
lines: climate weapons are being deployed in a
Climate War that all of us think is attributed to
global warming. Even if all of this is true, Kerry
could never admit it. I think we should take him
at his word. There's a new weapon of mass
destruction. The Climate Weapon. The rest,
terrorists and nukes, are just tools of deceit: tools
to disguise secret technologies that should not be
explained. For at least 19 years (since 1997), we
have been in a Climate War, or World War C.

Who has a Climate Weapon? My guess? Russia.

I don't deny climate change but neither do I
support it. Logic tells me that the Earth is far
more industrious than the best climatologist.
Plus, given the fact that Earth has survived for 4.5
billion years gives credence to the fact that
climate change experts are wildly delusional with
their facts and figures. Earth is not a fact and
figure. It is a 4.5 billion year old planetoid. If the
only thing protecting the planet from freezing and
overheating was carbon dioxide (or, greenhouse

gases) then my guess is that this planet would have melted a long time ago. The fact is that we don't know how this planet works but we need catchy words like "carbon" and "global warming" and "global cooling" to sell to the worshipers of the apocalypse. I don't believe in doomsdays. As much as I'm unorthodox in my thinking, I'm also a realist. I do believe we have weather weapons and they are being deployed.

Additionally, the presence of climate weapons comes with some other implications, and these I think are relevant. If John Kerry is aware of the weaponization of the weather over America, and he is the Secretary of State—among the highest in the Cabinet—then it can be understood that the former Secretary of State, Hillary Clinton, was also briefed on these matters on national security. This goes the same for the Secretary of Defense, William Cohen.

If the Obama Cabinet is aware of climate weapons, and they watch the weather channel, then the president is obviously aware. But we are going back to 1997 and we are in 2016—that's 19 years of Cabinet members who all knew about climate weapons. Barack Obama, Bill Clinton, George W. Bush (and likely George H. Bush)—all know about the power of weather manipulation. That's my guess. And they didn't tell anyone in the G8 meetings. Interestingly, weather modification was introduced to U.S. legislation in 2005 and 2007. According to Wikipedia, Beijing has a weather modification office. Well, so does Russia.

PART 3
Flight 370

CHAPTER 9

THE ODYSSEY OF FLIGHT 370

"Can it not be that the pilot of MH370 lost control of their aircraft after someone directly or remotely activated the equipment for seizure of control of the aircraft." ~ DR. MAHATHIR, FORMER PM OF MALAYSIA, MAY 18, 2014

A plane in the sky looks rather small. It appears to be the size of a giant bird. A bird with jet turbines is able to shuttle hundreds of passengers from one city to the next, across over vast amounts of water and reams of uninhabitable terrain. We rely on airplanes to make our lives convenient. Whether to keep a business meeting or to visit a family member, an airplane is a valued form of travel.

The Boeing Company is an $86 billion American manufacturing giant. Founded in 1916 by William

Boeing who wanted to build his own seaplanes, by 1958 the company had built its first commercial jetliner, the Boeing 707. By 1970, the four-engine 747 entered the market and changed air travel. The 777 was built as an advanced twin-jet commercial aircraft that featured electronic flight controls, fly-by-wire, avionics primarily run by computers.

Boeing not only manufactures commercial aircraft, the company also builds for the military and aerospace. The stealth B-2 bomber, space shuttle, and the International Space Station all have Boeing parts and designs. Boeing Defense, Space & Security (BDS) is the military and aerospace arm of Boeing. It builds fighter jets, unmanned aerial vehicles (UAVs), surveillance planes, and communications satellites.

In order to preserve the leadership during a national emergency, Boeing created the E-4B for the United States Air, a modified 747-200 with advanced electronics, advanced communications and electromagnetic shielding in case of a nuclear EMP attack. The E-4B can stay airborne from 2 days to a full week, in emergency situations. Did I say that the E-4B is equipped with advanced communications and EM shielding?

Electromagnetic shielding is one way for a plane to become invisible. It won't appear on any radar and it won't receive any satellite handshakes.

Extended flight operations were truly achieved with the orbital space vehicle, the X-37B, built by Boeing, NASA, and DARPA. A classified and unmanned spaceplane launched into low earth orbit via rockets, said to circle the Earth every 90 minutes. The first launch in April 2010 kept the spaceplane in orbit for 224 days. The second mission launched March 2011 and kept the X-37B in orbit for 469 days. December 2012 saw the third launch of this classified military orbital test vehicle (OTV). Dubbed by some a spy plane and cloaked in secrecy, it landed in October 2014, 674 days later.

On March 8, 2014, Malaysia Airlines Flight 370 began its odyssey into the history books of aviation disasters. I first wrote about MH370 about two weeks after it had disappeared and many of the discussions you find in this book pertain to that early prognosis, far ahead of any meaningful search and rescue operation. MH370 was a Boeing 777-200 ER (extended range) commercial airliner piloted by Captain Zaharie Ahmad Shah and First Officer Fariq Abdul Hamid.

The plane started out of Kuala Lumpur, Malaysia at 12:41 a.m. on March 8. There was nothing out of the ordinary. At 1:01 a.m. it reached cruising altitude of about 35,000 feet with nothing to report. It wasn't until the co-pilot said, "Good night, Malaysia three-seven-zero," between Malaysia Air Traffic Control (ATC) and Vietnam ATC at 1:19 a.m. that things started to become strange. For unknown reasons, two minutes later MH370 shut off multiple communications systems and military radar later showed that it made a U-turn back over the Malaysian peninsula, heading up over the tip of Sumatra and disappeared. No strange maneuvers. Not autopilot headings. No zig-zags or rapid descent. No emergency squawks due to aircraft hijacking. No distress signals from an explosion onboard. Both pilots had been checked out. All the passengers passed background checks. No calls recorded from the 200 mobile phones in passenger's pockets. No hijacker demands. Despite shutdown of independent communications systems, the plane continued to fly for another 6 hours, shown by records from Inmarsat, a British communications satellite that picked up hourly pings.

Search operations for MH370 have not found anything, so far, in a 23,000 square mile area in the southern Indian Ocean. The search zone is based on the proprietary data from the maintenance pings on the British-owned Inmarsat. On April 17, 2015, Australia's deputy prime minister, Warren Truss, and Liow Tiong Lai, the Malaysian transportation minister, said that the search area will be doubled to 46,000 square miles through the rest of 2015, raising the total cost to nearly $120 million.

That is the basic story of Flight 370. In terms of aviation analysis, the search and rescue teams started late due to miscommunication and then looked in the wrong places on the map. Experts were baffled by the complete failure of independent communications systems built on triple redundancy because it meant that all systems had to fail simultaneously which would indicate massive damage to the plane. It would make it highly unlikely that a severely crippled plane could continue to fly another 6 hours. Because the aircraft's flight controls were built on computer systems, a system called "fly-by-wire," it meant that a plane that had reached cruising altitude didn't really need a pilot. Had the plane been hijacked, either pilot would have alerted ATC or switched on any of the distress signals, they would have activated the anti-hijacking and anti-terrorist systems built into the 777.

I realize that in discussing some of the technical aspects of a Boeing 777, I may be extending my area of knowledge, and I'd like to apologize up front if my technical descriptions are less than perfect. That said, I think that the overall narrative such as the simultaneous loss of independent communications is accurate. Whether an aircraft can be tracked over the ocean and how satellites track it is beyond the level of my discussion. It also doesn't add to my exotic premise which is centered on MH370 as a tool to deescalate a brewing war between Russia and the United States. The loss of 239 passengers and crew is a tragedy. The potential loss of 100,000 civilians is a nightmare.

For the record, I'm not involved in any of the events I describe in this book, I only want to explain my theory that MH370 was professionally removed for reasons that the master thieves considered vital to maintaining international peace and cooperation. Whether the disappearance of an aircraft created a global media distraction or whether it bought time for politicians to negotiate better terms, we will never know.

What we do know is that the tension in the Ukraine and the Russian occupation of Crimea did not escalate into a war between Russia and the USA. If that was the intended goal, then you have to say that a major crisis had been averted. It should be clear that I do not know why Malaysia Airlines 370 was taken off the map. The world knows that the plane vanished. As of this writing, 15 months after the event, there are no answers to the mystery. I am also not saying that the hired professionals who reallocated the flight can do so at a whim. This event has the hallmark of strategy and tactics, and these I usually attribute to intelligence or military.

There was a mission and the mission apparently succeeded. The guts of the mission were morally ambiguous, again that is my observation, but the mission itself seems to have succeeded. There is no new war with Russia. My amateur analysis of the disappearing Flight 370, together with the other arguments in this book, tells me that there are clandestine operatives working in the background, for whatever reason, and their chief goal is to preserve our history as a species.

There are times when those missions fail as well as times when those covert operations are misused. The point that I take away from all of this is that there are ongoing covert operations and it is not a conspiracy theory. Flight 370 vanished into thin air. Is it gone? Malaysia Airlines Flight 17, also a Boeing 777, was shot down over Ukraine on July 17, 2014. Was Flight 17 and Flight 370 the same plane? The Russians blamed the Ukrainians. The Ukrainians blamed pro-Russian insurgents.

The loss of Flight 370 was a vital piece to a puzzle I had been working on since 2010, and it had to do with the deployment of climate weapons and the tragedy that woke me up was the Haiti earthquake. Other natural disasters followed (eg Hurricane Sandy and Polar Vortex) along with other earthquakes (eg Tohoku). Flight 370, in the manner the operation was executed, not only signified that covert operations were activated, more importantly it highlighted the deployment of advanced weather machines. And if weather weapons have been regularly deployed across this planet, for whatever reasons, then the public needs to be alerted to this important fact. Not only that, but climatologists should be particularly interested in knowing that climate statistics are grossly inaccurate and long-range weather forecasts (ie global warming) are woefully mismanaged because they do not take into account technologies that can modify the weather.

CHAPTER 10

OVERRIDING PILOT CONTROLS

"We tried multiple times to get information from Boeing on this project. The company would not speak to us about it." ~ BRIAN TODD, CNN CORRESPONDENT, MARCH 28, 2014

In the age of computerized flight systems and unmanned aerial vehicles, hijackers are no longer needed to be onboard a plane to commandeer an aircraft. We are seeing this with the massive use of military and hobby drones. A "pilot" need only reside inside of a room with a computer, a satellite link, and a few logon passwords. Drone enthusiasts fly using remote controls. It turns out that the Boeing 777 had (likely) built-in anti-hijacking systems whereby a pilot on the ground could remotely takeover the plane, locking out the pilot, and flying the plane virtually to any location they wanted. And by means of activating another program, the plane would land on a foreign runway all by itself. Call it modern day aircraft hijacking.

When CNN Correspondent Brian Todd reported on the 2004 Boeing patent for the "uninterruptible autopilot" system, Boeing refused to talk about it. This anti-hijacking system could allow a plane to be remotely flown much like an unmanned drone. It could be navigated to an airstrip and landed by computer. Unfortunately, this kind of system could be hacked. Such a plane could be forced to land elsewhere. What we can understand from deployable technology that went through the patent system in 2004 is that this technology goes through rigorous testing. That is to say, tested during actual flights. Because you can only do so much under controlled conditions. These "test" autopilot systems would be added without any passenger knowledge. In fact, we could infer that certain planes had this system built-in, and could be activated if needed. We might also add that a patent in 2004 had gone through 10 to 15 years of development.

While Dr. Mahathir may have a point that the CIA and Boeing aren't talking. Patents do exist for systems that can deactivate on-board flight controls. One U.S. patent (No. 6,641,087 B1), assigned to Cubic Defense Systems in November 2003, apparently is designed to work with any plane with an autopilot system in place. In a basic configuration (of many), a manager at a remote ground facility is alerted by a panic button in the cockpit. The manager then gets access to the plane's avionics and can take command of the plane. This is done through a transceiver device installed on the plane. In dire emergencies, even the flight recorder data can be downloaded through the transceiver.

If you have a remote link facility or an available satellite, it is entirely possible to lock out the pilots and takeover the plane. "In general, the invention counteracts otherwise successful hijackings by forcibly assuming control of the aircraft, and overriding pilot controls in the cockpit." This invention is dated 2003, at least partially inspired by the terrorist attacks on 9/11. An option on this system is a feature that can disable all communications systems. Additionally, the remote guidance station needn't be on the ground "as such equipment may be in airborne flight, orbit, or other non-ground site."

The technology to remotely control a commercial jetliner has been around for at least 15 years, and has very likely been implemented and undisclosed for national security reasons. A lot of the advancements in electronic flight systems, such as fly-by-wire, have granted additional flight authority to anyone with computer and a satellite relay. You wouldn't need to hack into a commercial jet because it most likely comes equipped with anti-hijacking systems if only that means installing a secret transceiver onboard, and the transceiver these days could be the size of a handheld USB drive. Cellphones and tablet PCs have transceivers. We're not talking science fiction here in case anyone was thinking that. We are talking about a technical aptitude that most people don't have.

The other main idea to consider is that nearly every computer system, especially on an airplane, has at least one modem, which is a transceiver-receiver and a modem can be dialled through a satellite, with the right codes. Again, I'm not a technical wizard and neither do I want to scare people. What I want to do, because some people think this is science fiction, is to let you understand that it isn't difficult for a professional to remote-jack a plane. The problem is that this sort of thing is frowned up on in the media and is not an ideal topic of discussion because it might frighten the audience. Flying is one of the safest modes of travel there is, it just so happened that Flight 370 *needed* to be taken.

When we talked about the Boeing Company we also mentioned that they built aircraft for the military and aerospace, and one such aircraft, the E-4B—a staffed airborne command and control 747 plane—could fly around up to one week. If one of these planes had a remote guidance facility, not a difficult task and within the capacity of modern warfare, and had been flying high enough—being *undetectable* because of its electromagnetic shielding—one aircraft would be all that is required to remote-jack MH370. This scenario would neither be detected nor admitted, in effect satisfying most of the mysterious elements of this airborne odyssey.

Additionally, there is the X-37B, an unmanned spaceplane that can stay in space for 2 years. It too is equipped with all kinds of communications and surveillance equipment, except we don't know exactly what kind of equipment because the X-37B is highly classified. This is the unmanned version of a remote-jack scenario.

How far back does remote flying go? In the movie *Hangar 18*, starring Darren McGavin, about the recovery of a damaged alien spacecraft. The government, in an effort to destroy the evidence of alien friendship, *remotely flies a*

plane loaded with explosives into the hangar.
The movie was released in 1980.

The ability to remote fly an aircraft, even
without the fly-by-wire system, has been around
for at least 40 years, conservatively. Boeing itself
patented an anti-terrorist system in November
2006 (Patent: US 7,142, 971 B2), and in 2004
according to CNN. Control of the plane can be
done remotely by "disconnecting the onboard
controls and/or providing uninterruptible power
to the automatic control system." Through the
engagement of an "uninterruptible autopilot
mode" the aircraft can be remotely navigated to
another location. All that is needed is a
communication link.

Boeing has never confirmed whether the patents
were ever implemented. It would be in Boeing's
interest to have anti-hijacking systems, if even for
maintenance issues and test flights, on a modern
aircraft. And the technological know-how for all
intents and purposes has been around since at
least 1980 through the military or the intelligence
agencies. The paradox of a vanishing plane could
be simply answered, but that perhaps is not an
answer people want to hear.

This situation sort-of reminds me of the film,
Life of Pi, whereby a shipwrecked Indian boy
must survive alongside a Bengal tiger that had

devoured a zebra, an orangutan, and a hyena on the lifeboat. Pi, the boy, survives the trek to the coast of Mexico, where the tiger departs peacefully. When interviewed, Pi tells two stories to the insurance agents. The first, with the animals. But the agents don't believe him. So he tells them a second story: this one with the zebra standing for a crewmember, the orangutan standing for his mother, and the hyena standing for a violent cook. Pi killed the cook and lived off of his flesh. The agents, and later a novelist who interviews him, prefer the first story. "And so it goes with God," said an adult Pi.

CHAPTER 11

HOW TO MAKE A PLANE DISAPPEAR

How do you make a commercial jetliner disappear and then to steer it off course? You need three things:

1. A compliant pilot
2. A method to cloak the airplane to evade detection
3. A method to commandeer a Boeing 777

The best way to achieve a compliant pilot is *activate* a sleeping agent, aka Manchurian candidate, and to upload the new data into his hippocampus, the memory center. Activation isn't difficult, a code word by phone, a symbolic gesture from a stranger, a certain email. All of this follows a number of months in prep, which could include running automated flight scenarios on the home-built flight simulator. The activation of a Manchurian candidate ensures compliance. You need compliance in order to coordinate the rest of the mission objectives.

Once Malaysia Airlines aircraft was well on its way and had reached cruising altitude, that was when the transponder was turned off and communications were cut. Flight 370 is unique in the sense that not only did the transporter get turned off, and it did have a switch, but other vital communications equipment were cut, including ACARS and ELT (emergency locator transmitter), among other equipment. What is interesting about ACARS is that to disable it fully requires considerable access to the electronics panel underneath the cockpit.

In addition to those, depending on the configuration, there are at least several ELT devices; one of them is in the tail of the plane. Some are also on the slide rafts. ELTs can be activated by a crew member but also are automatically activated in salt water, and in crashes. No ELT device has been picked up by any monitoring device so far. That would mean that the plane did not crash into the ocean. If the plane crashed on land, other transmitters might have activated.

How does the crew, or a hijacker for that matter, disable all the communication systems, given the fact that not all of them are available and accessible? One solution is to hit the plane with an electromagnetic beam (electronic warfare), not enough to knock out the electronics, but just enough to scramble all communication channels, even to make it appear that systems were "shut off." And this was the regular analysis of the communication systems among panel after panel of aviation experts on CNN.

I watched and listened to many hours of technical discussions on Flight 370 and one of the mysteries of the plane's disappearance had to do with the almost simultaneous and deliberate shut down of the communication systems, making the plane vanish into thin air. "The perpetrators—and I will call them perpetrators—were deliberately obfuscating their intentions and so you have a particularly tricky set of problems," said Jeff Wise, aviation journalist and private pilot, to Erin Burnett, host of CNN's *OutFront,* on March 21, 2014. My explanation rests on a military satellite in the area, which there are many, and enough of an electromagnetic signal to *temporarily shut off* communication equipment onboard, which is all based on radio frequencies, and this makes for an improvised cloaking device.

The pilot, or even hijacker, it doesn't matter, only needs to provide a few functions—fly the jet out of Kuala Lumpur, reach cruising altitude, turn off the transponder, and then input the data for a new destination, as examples—after that, a third party military contractor scrambles communications and cloaks the plane from basic forms of detection. What's next?

The next thing you need to do is to commandeer the jetliner and to deliver it to your specific ends. Recall in the televised discussions on Flight 370, there had been no demands from any terrorist group and for all intents and purposes, both the pilot and co-pilot did not show any terrorist intentions. All the passengers were reported to not be connected to any terrorist groups.

In other words, there was no motive to steal this plane. There was no one accountable. And, generally speaking from my experience, a tragedy without motive, and if it wasn't a freak accident, often points to a "designed event." I think the disappearance of Malaysia Airlines Flight 370 is one of those kinds of events. A *designed event* is launched for a specific purpose, which we will discuss.

When aviation experts and pilots were asked if the aircraft's computer system could have been remotely hacked, all of them insisted that it was virtually unthinkable; today their minds may have changed. Maybe it's not the kind of thing that most people can do, but if Snowden can download thousands of documents from the most secure computer networks in the world, at National Intelligence, then it is also the case that there are people who can hack into a Boeing's anti-hijacking system, specifically people who either have access to the password or those who are just good at computer science and have free access to a military satellite.

By insisting on a military satellite being involved in the crime, I am also suggesting that some kind of military agency was involved, and since this kind of military would not likely belong to any one particular nation, I would have to conclude that this military agency is some kind of contractor, perhaps even mercenaries who work for a fee. And all they would need is some kind of Boeing E-4B aircraft, perhaps a custom-made module. This airborne remote guidance facility can be fully staffed or unmanned, or any combination thereof.

Since I don't know for certain, I'll assume that this Boeing 777 came with an anti-hijacking system (or, had a communication link that could be used to access the onboard flight computers). Boeing patented a new anti-hijacking system in

2004 and 2006. This system had the power to lockout the pilots and to assume full control of the aircraft, and since the aircraft is primarily computerized, anyone with access to this anti-hijacking system could fly this aircraft "as if" they were in the cockpit.

They could fly up to 45,000 feet and knock out all the passengers from *hypoxia*, for example, since they themselves would be remotely located somewhere else, and with plenty of oxygen, even a fresh cup of coffee. Once the plane's occupants were unconscious and with full control of a cloaked aircraft, the destiny of that plane would be certain.

One of the implications in my hypothesis, and this is what it is (for now), is that the persons responsible for this mystery have been careful not to leave any fingerprints. These are professionals. These are ex-military. These are expert pilots. These guys are specialists. They've done this before. Remember, the military has been trained to take out enemy aircraft communications during an engagement. The military have been trained to hack into aircraft computers and to remote fly the planes. Even intelligence operatives can be trained for this sort of thing. We're seeing this remote flying with drones. Same technology. Same set of skills. One of the easiest ways to hack into the aircraft computers without anyone knowing is to dial a modem and use the password. That's all you need.

So, you activate your Manchurian pilot, making sure they are in accordance with the mission. Once their actions are complete, and the blame is attributable to that action, that's when the professionals move in and take over. What separates a good thief from a master thief is that the master thief was never near the crime scene and the good thief left his DNA on the seat cushion. The pilots of MH370 provided all the fingerprints to cover, or mask, the actions of the thieves, or master thieves, or just people who have an enviable access to advanced technologies.

Once the ship is remote-controlled and expertly cloaked from detection, and provided that military eyes in the region don't want to squander their military capabilities unnecessarily, then that zombie aircraft becomes the headlines of the day. Of every day. For weeks, everyone was talking about MH370 and very few were ever concerned about the new Cold War with Russia. Remember the Cold War? Most people had forgotten because all they saw in the news was the search for Flight 370.

"Will we ever find the plane?" asked Burnett to her panel of CNN experts on March 21, 2014.

Miles O'Brien, broadcast journalist and aviation analyst, responded, "Maybe." Broadcast journalist and aviation analyst following this story Richard Quest said, "They won't stop looking." Aviation journalist Jeff Wise said, "I think there's a good chance that it'll find us." Aviation attorney Arthur Rosenberg said, "I don't think we are going to find this plane, or any part of it, for *a while*."

With the much-needed media attention and hype required to launch an improvised Cold War, which was essentially their whole plan since the era of the Cold War was long dead, whoever was behind the Cold War lost all momentum and the window of opportunity was mostly, but not completely, lost. Found or not found Flight MH370 stole the stage, so to speak.

CHAPTER 12

A NEW COVERT OPERATION

While I don't know what happened to the passengers of MH370 (how can I?) my best guess is that they have been sequestered, dead or alive, in some remote location. Even if alive, they cannot be returned to the real world. It is plausible they might be lifted offplanet. In any case, no one can know what really happened. And that's the basis for a book like this. It's not a book on a conspiracy. It's not weird fiction. It's an incomplete yet provocative explanation to an exotic crime, a crime which appears to have been necessary. Was it a necessary crime? Was the occupation of Crimea necessary? In my world view, necessary events happen all the time. Some events cover other events which in turn cover other events.

False flag events have been documented across recent history, even admitted ones. A false flag is a covert operation whereby the group behind the operation is concealed by a group carrying out the operation. A false flag typically creates a necessary reaction without any accountability. It's as simple as a soldier who dresses up in an enemy uniform and carries out an attack on the enemy. The enemy is attacked by one of its own people and the soldier's army may or may never be realized. War is deception. It works.

Operation Northwoods, 1962, during the Kennedy Administration, included hijacking passenger planes and sinking US ships only to blame Cuba, a plan to overthrow Castro. The Gulf of Tonkin incident, 1964, where the destroyer USS Maddox was attacked by North Vietnamese torpedo boats, which led Lyndon B. Johnson to legally deploy forces against the Vietcong, never happened. Former US Secretary of Defense, Robert McNamara, admitted it. Declassified NSA documents in 2005, 40 years later, indicated that the incident used to justify the war didn't happen. The North Vietnamese never attacked America's ships.

The MH370 incident will turn out to be yet another covert operation. The 2013 coup d'état in the Ukraine will be included as a related incident.

I'm not a conspiracy theorist. I've developed my own system of analysis and I use it for exotic events and discoveries. This kind of thinking should not be used liberally. It works on very complex, multilayered, and intricate events. And it doesn't work perfectly. There's simply no way to have all the answers unless you're on the team that masterminded the event and those people will never talk, if history is any example.

You have to respect the fact that these kinds people are in the world, that they look like anybody, and that they are able to do things that most people would find unimaginable (and controversial). You only hope that they are guided by a higher sense of morality, and should any of them slip off the exotic boat, they should be rounded up in an efficient fashion.

Plus, by the time any truth is declassified it'll have been 40 years, most of the people who followed the event are either dead or too old to remember. So the revelation is without any real fanfare. So my view is that if my explanation is relatively accurate, given the intricate challenges of this event, but if my explanation is good then it is possible that this explanation may survive history and children and grandchildren may care what happened to MH370.

PARIS TOSEN

FINAL ARGUMENTS

CHAPTER 13

THE LANGUAGE OF CLIMATE BOMBS

Russia antagonizes America with a hard winter. Starting in November 2013. That very same month, the United States antagonizes Russia with a revolution in Ukraine, an old ally of the Russian Federation. Both of those actions have either a covert, or clandestine, nature, ie they're hard to prove. But the actions themselves, as evidence, are easy to see. America is hit with an unprecedented winter that even weather experts can't properly explain and the Ukraine, with a pro-Moscow leader, collapses in a matter of months.

  These two actions—Arctic storms and Ukraine collapse—lead to a third action: a Russian invasion of Ukraine, starting with the Crimean Peninsula. On the verge of a new Russian war, directly caused be a Perkins-style coup d'état in a neighboring nation, there's this plane that disappears off the face of the Earth and has 25 countries scouring 3 million square miles for it. Search teams eventually settle on a 46,000 square mile area. More than two years later, not a trace of the plane.

And what is everyone concerned about? Is it the manipulated war with Russia and its 25,000 troops on the borders of Ukraine or is it the tragedy of Malaysia Airlines Flight 370 and the 239 onboard?

The answer is MH370, isn't it? Two weeks of Front Page news.

That's enough to de-escalate a manipulated war. But wait a minute—it's all manipulated. The Polar Vortex is a manipulation. The coup in Ukraine is a manipulation. Even Edward Snowden—do we really think that he acted alone? Remember about the master thief? The master thief leaves no fingerprints. Did Snowden indirectly trigger a clash between two superpowers?

What truly motivated a 29-year-old man in Hawaii into tossing his $122,000 income and subverting his entire government? Not his conscience. Because if it was his conscience, as he himself insists, then out of the 50,000 or so NSA employees, we would've seen at least 100 of them stepping into the spotlight after all these years. Or at least a dozen. Instead what we have is NSA veteran William Binney speaking out in 2001 and Edward Snowden in 2013.

In all likelihood, Snowden was used to derail the unconstitutional mass surveillance of Americans, but Snowden's escape was cut off prematurely and he happened to find refuge with an old American enemy, Russia, who didn't mind that Snowden had released documents that hurt the U.S. Administration. The CIA was also involved in helping Snowden in Russia, for example former senior CIA analyst and Russian-speaking Ray McGovern considered Snowden a whistleblower, and that meant the CIA was concerned about the NSA and civil liberties. To get Snowden, the U.S. Administration pressured the Kremlin—and the Kremlin pushed back. In order to de-escalate an imminent military conflict, a passenger jet was masterfully taken off the map.

Where do we go with all of this? What do we do with the knowledge that beneath the public façade hides an even more sinister hand? Was it right to take 239 lives; instead of the tens of thousands of lives that might've been taken had a war broke out? These are both moral and philosophical questions that you'll have to answer for yourself. My argument is that Malaysia Airlines Flight 370 vanished, and because it vanished, the United States and Russia are not at war.

If you were to ask me further, I would speculate that Edward Snowden's actions against his government was a giant slap into the face of the Obama Administration. When Saddam Hussein refused to cooperate with the Bush Administration, his nation was invaded and Saddam executed. A 29-year-old guy robs America of its secrets and gets away? Not only that but he finds shelter in the arms of an enemy superpower? I'd say President Obama showed a lot restraint. Or maybe not. The CIA took out the pro-Russian Ukrainian leader. Putin reacted with a winter storm and the occupation of Crimea. It later would take three earthquakes in Orange County to get Obama to take Putin's phone call. And while the politics brewed on the stove of democracy, everyone's eyes were glued to the fate of the Malaysia Airlines passengers and crew.

That was the main argument of the first edition of this book. Indeed, there was secondary argument, a provocative hypothesis having to with a Climate War between these same two superpowers. The presence of a Climate War exposed the operation of climate bombs, the latest in military equipment. Not for sale to the general public.

Turns out, climate change is man-made—by people who understand environmental biology, geology, seismology, and physics; and do not adhere to laws, morality, or transparency. Climatologists paranoid about the rising greenhouse gases (a catchy term for carbon dioxide in the atmosphere) and obsessed with CO_2 statistics see the swath of severe storms, earthquakes and droughts and they begin to become even more paranoid about trapped carbon in our atmosphere.

What they fail to see is that some of these natural disasters, especially the severe ones, have nothing to do with carbon and everything to do with electromagnetic climate bombs. Climate scientists who do not factor man-made weather modification are misleading the public and until now no climate scientist has ever factored in artificial weather modification, if only because it has never been (properly) made public.

When climatologists see frequent large earthquakes, winter storms, droughts, hurricanes, and other extreme weather they will take that as a *sign* that their global warming theory is true when these weather events have nothing to do with global warming. While an earthquake may not be blamed on global warming, a heat wave will. It is a fact that climate scientists general believe that extreme weather and global warming go together.

My argument, if climate weapons do exist, is that extreme weather conditions have nothing to do with any global warming theory. A Hurricane Katrina and Hurricane Sandy can be generated with the right electromagnetic punch. Then why push Climate Change? Two words: cover story. You can't have an on-going climate war without climate change because people will think it's the end of the world. So you ease public paranoia, and put people to sleep with a little lie.

Understanding climate weapons and their ability to create extreme weather events is an entirely new language, a language so new and offensive that it will turn off many people at the outset. It's no different than an illiterate person visiting the New York Library and its 53 million materials or a person who cannot fathom why a Jackson Pollock painting (No 5, 1948) could sell for $140 million.

Climate bombs are so powerful they can knock out entire cities without a moment's notice. To disregard and dismiss these constructed events would only lead to the defeat of the world public. We forget that America's deployment of two nuclear weapons validated a new cultural hegemony, a military superpower and no end to war. Likewise, I insist, the deployment of climate bombs through advanced electromagnetic weapon systems is going to lead to a defeat of old war technologies and might one day become the representative weapon of military superpowers. Verily, one of these classes of weapons in the wrong hands could change the geopolitical landscape overnight. We are seeing first-hand demonstrations of titanic weapons that once only belonged to gods like Zeus and Thor. Until now, we haven't had the language to read climate attacks. I hope that from now on you will pay more attention to weather events.

Our climate has been weaponized and the human race needs to become mobilized.

Notes

Preface

CNN provided wall-to-wall news coverage of the disappearance of Malaysia Flight 370. Guests on the show were aviation experts. These people included: aviation expert Richard Quest, safety and accident investigator David Soucie, former managing director of the National Transportation Safety Board Peter Goelz, aviation analyst Les Abend, aviation and space journalist Miles O'Brien, aviation lawyer and safety advocate Mary Schiavo, and private pilot and science writer Jeff Wise.

David Soucie's book on the subject is *Malaysia Airlines Flight 370: Why It Disappeared — and Why It's Only a Matter of Time Before This Happens Again* (Skyhorse Publishing, 2015).

Richard Quest, who was photographed with the pilot of MH370 only weeks before it disappeared, presents his take on the airline mystery in *The Vanishing of Flight MH370: The True Story of the Hunt for the Missing Malaysia Plane* (Berkley, 2016).

An early conspiracy theory on MH370 came from one of CNN's experts. Jeff Wise believed that Putin ordered the plane hijacked and the hijackers "spoofed" the flight data. "Vladimir Putin Ordered Russian Special Forces to Steal MH370 and Secretly Landed It at Huge Space Port in Kazakhstan, Claims Expert," DailyMail.com, March 4, 2015.

Sara C. Nelson, "MH370 was Hijacked on Vladimir Putin's Orders and Flown to Kazakhstan Says Aviation Expert Jeff Wise," *Huffington Post UK*, February 25, 2015. Retrieved at www.huffingtonpost.co.uk/2015 /02/25/mh370-hijacked-vladimir-putins-orders-flown-kazakhstan-aviation-expert-jeff-wise_n_6750148.htm.

Just so that we are all on the same wavelength, I have built my self-published book catalogue out of alternative thinking and rogue research on usually highly controversial topics, such as my book *God is DNA*. Had the plane disappeared without the other elements at play, the anomalous weather events, Edward Snowden and the America-Russia cold war—I would not have taken any interest in writing this book. In other words, the plane is another piece of a very complicated puzzle. Seeing that my perspective could at some point in the future alleviate many unanswered questions, I felt compelled to delve into topics that I am not normally familiar with. Because my strength had everything to do with exotic events, those that are inexplicable and controversial, and I have developed a skill at looking into controversial mysteries.

Chapter 1: A cold war brews on the stove of democracy

The flight of Edward Snowden became world news in 2013. This is a good summary of whistleblower Snowden, "Latest on the Computer Analyst Whistleblower Who Provided the *Guardian* with Top-Secret NSA Documents Leading to Revelations About US Surveillance on Phone and Internet Communications," www.theguardian.com/us-news/edward-snowden. Barton Gellman, "Edward Snowden, After Months of NSA Revelations, Says His Mission's Accomplished," *Washington Post*, December 23, 2013.

His actions blindsided the Obama Administration, which then went out to cripple his escape and rein him back to the United States. But that didn't happen. Here is Snowden in an interview by the *Guardian* on June 17, 2013:

I imagine everyone's experience is different, but for me, there was no single moment. It was seeing a continuing litany of lies from senior officials to Congress - and therefore the American people - and the realization that that Congress, specifically the Gang of Eight, wholly supported the lies that compelled me to act. Seeing someone in the position of James Clapper - the Director of National Intelligence - baldly lying to the public without repercussion is the evidence of a subverted democracy. The consent of the governed is not consent if it is not informed.

Chapter 2: Ukraine in winter

The revolution in Ukraine is an integral component of the argument and ties directly to Russian's involvement. In February 2010, Viktor Yanukovych became the president of Ukraine. On November 21, 2013, President Yanukovych chooses closer ties to Russia rather than the EU. This is the beginning of a year-long revolution. "Ukraine Crisis: Timeline," www.bbc.com/news.

"Ukraine Suspends Preparations for EU Trade Agreement," BBC.com, November 21, 2013.

WORLD WAR C

David M. Herszenhorn, "Ukraine in Turmoil After Leaders Reject Major E.U. Deal," *New York Times*, November 26, 2013. Retrieved at www.nytimes.com/2013/11/27/world/europe /protests-continue-as-ukraine-leader-defends-stance-on-europe.htm.

Blake Neff, "Putin says US backed a Coup d'État in Ukraine," *Hill*, May 23, 2014. www.thehill.com.

Record low temperatures hit the US in late 2013, turning into a "Polar Vortex" by the beginning of 2014. Alan Duke, "Frigid Air from the North Pole: What's this Polar Vortex?" CNN.com, January 6, 2014.

Wikipedia does a good job of covering the storm that set record low temperatures across eastern coast of North America. Early 2014 North American Cold Wave. (n.d.). In *Wikipedia*. Retrieved on June 25, 2016, from https://en.wikipedia.org/wiki/Early_2014_North_American_col d_wave. When describing the impact on the United States, we find:

> Evan Gold of weather intelligence firm Planalytics called the storm and the low temperatures the worst weather event for the economy since Hurricane Sandy just over a year earlier. 200 million people were affected, and Gold calculated the impact at $5 billion. $50 to $100 million was lost by airlines which cancelled a total of 20,000 flights after the storm began on January 2.

The NSA files: The *Guardian* discussing spying on citizens and state surveillance, www.theguardian.com/us-news/the-nsa-files.

Transcript, interview with President Barack Obama, *The Tonight Show with Jay Leno*, NBC, August 7, 2013.

The former NSA officer is portrayed in a film, Snowden, by filmmaker Oliver Stone. "Oliver Stone Reveals Details About His 'Snowden' Biopic," Rhonda Richford, Hollywood Reporter, June 22, 2016, viewed at www.hollywoodreporter.com/news. Stone said of the film: "It's a ten year story starting in the military and going to the point where he releases the stories."

Borman, M. (Producer), & Stone, O. (Director). (2016). *Snowden* [Motion Picture]. United States: Open Road Films.

John Perkins does an impressive job explaining how paid professionals are used to put poor countries into debt, *Confessions of an Economic Hit Man* (Plume, 2005).

"Confessions of an Economic Hit Man: How the U.S. Uses Globalization to Cheat Poor Countries Out of Trillions," www.democracynow.org/2004/11/9/confessions_of_an_econom ic_hit_man, November 9, 2004.

2003 Invasion of Iraq. (n.d.). In *Wikipedia*. Retrieved on June 25, 2016, from https://en.wikipedia.org/wiki/2003_invasion_of_Iraq.

David Hirst, "Saddam Hussein," *Guardian*, December 30, 2006. www.theguardian.com.

Paul Kirby, "Russia's Gas Fight with Ukraine," BBC.com, October 31, 2014.

Chapter 3: The makings of world war c

The Robert McNamara quote comes from Morris, E. (Producer), & Morris, E. (Director). (2003). *The Fog of War: Eleven Lessons from the Life of Robert S. McNamara* [Motion Picture]. United States: Sony Pictures Classics.

U.S. Secretary of State John Kerry equated climate change to a weapon of mass destruction. "John Kerry Warns Climate Change is 'the World's Most Fearsome Weapon of Mass Destruction,'" Dailymail.co.uk, February 17, 2014. Retrieved at www.democracynow.org/2004/11/9/confessions_ of_an_economic_hit_man.

Steve Almasy, "John Kerry: Climate Change as Big a Threat as Terrorism, Poverty, WMDs," CNN.com, February 17, 2014.

Arshad Mohammed, "John Kerry: Climate Change is 'Perhaps the World's Most Fearsome Weapon of Mass Destruction,'" Huffingtonpost.com, April 18, 2014. Retrieved at www.huffingtonpost.com /2014/02/16/john-kerry-climate-change_n_4798963.htm.

The story of stealing a weather machine from the US government is from Season 2 of *The Bionic Woman*. Rowe, A. (Writer), & Crosland Jr, A. (Director). (1976). *Kill Oscar*. [Episode 5]. Kenneth J. (Producer), *The Bionic Woman*. ABC. October 27, 1976. Television. It continues in Episode 6, *Kill Oscar: Part 3*, November 3, 1976. Television. Of note, former OSI scientist, Dr. Franklin (masterfully played by John Houseman), plans to clone OSI staff with fembots, android women, and then to steal the weather machine. While I enjoyed *Bionic Woman* and *Six Million Dollar Man* as a kid, I had never imagined that androids and weather machines might actually be real in the future. Ironic.

The movie that kicked off the climate change paranoia was David, L. (Producer), Guggenheim, D. (Director), Gore, A. (Actor). (2006). *An Inconvenient Truth* [Motion Picture]. United States: Paramount Classics. When the premise of a documentary combines a former Vice President of the United States (served during the Clinton administration, 1993-2001) who has a "lifelong commitment to reversing the effects of global climate change" and the science to justify the global warming theory, you know that you are in for a shakeup. This is kind of like Al Pacino in a documentary about changing the gun control laws in the United States or Joseph Stalin doing a documentary on how to save the dolphins. "Should we prepare for other threats besides terrorists?" is a quote from Gore's film. *An Inconvenient Truth* also earned Gore a Nobel Peace Prize (2007), a 2007 Grammy (Best Spoken Word Album), and the runner-up position for Time's Person of the Year in 2007 (Vladimir Putin won). We might think of 2006 as the launch of the Climate Change paranoia, that is, it wouldn't be important today without Al Gore. We could also say that climate change wouldn't exist without Al Gore. And we could say that climate change was invented.

A comprehensive discussion on the fight against climate change is from Naomi Klein, *This Changes Everything: Capitalism vs. the Climate* (Knopf, 2014). "Schemes for deliberately intervening in the climate system to counteract the effects of global warming have been around for half a century at least. In fact, when the President's Science Advisory Committee issued a report warning Lyndon B. Johnson about climate change in 1965, the authors made no mention of cutting emissions," page 261.

Jason Taylor, "'Global Warming the Greatest Scam in History' claims founder of the Weather Channel," Express.co.uk, June 10, 2015. Retrieved at www.express.co.uk/news/clarifications-corrections/526191/Climate-change-is-a-lie-global-warming-not-real-claims-weather-channel-founder.

"Where is the warming that we were promised?" is at the crux of the article by Levi Winchester, "'Where's the Global Warming? Expert Says Public are Growing Sceptical of Climate Change," Express.co.uk, October 6, 2014.

For good summaries of HAARP (High-Frequency Active Auroral Research Program) have a look at Rosalie Bertell's article, "Background of the HAARP Project," www.theforbiddenknowledge.com/ hardtruth

/haarp_mind_weather_control.htm; Nick Begich and Jeane
Manning, "The Military's Pandora's Box," www.haarp.net.

Nick Begich and Jeane Manning have looked at HAARP and
other electromagnetic weapons in *Angels Don't Play This Haarp:
Advances in Tesla Technology* (Earthpulse, 1995).

Record rainfall hit southern Alberta in mid-June 2013. Janet
Davison and Lucas Powers, "Why Alberta's Floods Hit So Hard
and Fast," CBC.ca, June 22, 2013. "To have these very large flood
events…the stars have to line up." The weather anomaly at
Environment and Climate Change Canada, "Canada's Top Ten
Weather Stories for 2013," www.ec.gc.ca. You might not like my
term Climate Bomb, which I invented as a way to describe the
highly anomalous weather, but I am not alone in this term. "So it
was no surprise that the water bomb that hit on June 19 wreaked
havoc."

June was a busy month for NSA agent Edward Snowden, a
whistleblower who found himself talking to journalist Glenn
Greenwald about the national-but-secret U.S. mass surveillance
program. The first story was published on June 5, 2013, followed
in succession by other stories. "That piece, detailing a secret court
order issued in April 2013 that compelled Verizon to hand over
consumer data to the NSA." Janet Reitman, "Snowden and
Greenwald: The Men Who Leaked the Secrets," *Rolling Stone*,
December 4, 2013. Retrieved at www.rollingstone.com.

The prophet of the Snowden Revelations, Glenn Greenwald,
continued to remain in the limelight while he published more of
the cache of NSA secrets. Michael Paterniti, "The Man Who
Knows Too Much," GQ.com, May 11, 2014.

Kim Ann Zimmermann, "Hurricane Katrina: Facts, Damage &
Aftermath," Livescience.com, August 27, 2015. "Katrina Was the
Most Destructive Storm to Strike the United States and the
Costliest Storm in U.S. History, Causing $108 Billion in Damage,
According to the National Oceanic and Atmospheric
Administration (NOAA)."

Olivier Laurent, "Haiti Earthquake: Five Years After,"
Time.com, January 12, 2015. The earthquake that struck Haiti on
January 12, 2010 killed 220,000 to 316,000 lives. Numbers could be
inflated. It had over 50 aftershocks. Short summary, CNN Library,
"Haiti Earthquake Fast Facts," CNN.com, December 13, 2015.

Becky Oskin, "Japan Earthquake & Tsunami of 2011: Facts and Information," Livescience.com, May 7, 2015. It was on March 11, 2011 when northeastern Japan felt the effects of a great earthquake, a magnitude-9. The strike caused a level 7 nuclear meltdown at the Fukushima Daiichi Nuclear Power Plant. "The shaking lasted about six minutes." For a good set of devastation photos look at Alan Taylor, "5 Years Since the 2011 Great East Japan Earthquake," *Atlantic*, March 10, 2016. www.theatlantic.com

Chapter 4: The weather bomb

"The Atomic Bombing of Hiroshima" and "The Atomic Bombing of Nagasaki," U.S. Department of Energy, www.osti.gov, provides a good summary of the fateful attacks on Japan on August 6 and August 9, 1945. Hiroshima had an estimated 43,000 soldiers. It was hit by the uranium bomb, *Little Boy*. "The yield of the explosion was later estimated at 15 kilotons (the equivalent of 15,000 tons of TNT)." The initial blast took 70,000 lives, but the effects of radiation would claim over 200,000 lives. *Fat Man*, a plutonium bomb, was dropped on the city of Nagasaki. "The yield of the explosion was later estimated at 21 kilotons, 40 percent greater than that of the Hiroshima bomb." Over 140,000 lives were lost. The two cities in Japan represent the only times in history where atomic bombs were used to take human lives. Japan surrendered on August 15, 1945. A little more than two weeks later, on September 2, World War II ended.

A good description of the Richter scale is Penn State University's online "Earth 520: Plate Tectonics and People," www.e-education.psu.edu/earth520.

Charles Richter wanted to be able to measure all types of earthquakes and so invented the Richter scale to measure the ground motion amplitude. Each point on the scale signified a factor of 10. But, Richter's work was specifically for the state of California. More recently, scientists are using "moment magnitude" (M_w) to describe an earthquake, with keeping the scale association to the Richter scale.

$$M_w = (2/3) * \log M_0 - 6.05$$

According to U.S. Geological Survey (USGS), the magnitude 9.0 earthquake that hit Sumatra released "475,000 kilotons (475 megatons) of TNT, or the equivalent of 23,000 Nagasaki bombs." Both nuclear blasts and earthquakes release energy. Earthquakes release stored energy from tectonic strain that builds up over time.

The 5-second Afghanistan earthquake in 1998 equalled the detonation of a 2,000 kiloton bomb. www.usgs.gov.

Find a chart at "What is the Energy of an Earthquake?" found at www.openhazards.com.

Australian Government, Bureau of Meteorology, "The Eruption of Krakatoa, August 27, 1883," www.bom.gov.au.

National Centers for Environmental Information (NOAA), "December 26, 2004 Sumatra Indonesia Earthquake and Tsunami," www.ngdc.noaa.gov.

Hannah Osborne, "2004 Indian Ocean Earthquake and Tsunami: Facts About the Boxing Day Disaster," *International Business Times*, December 22, 2014. www.ibtimes.co.uk.

A copy of the Treaty on the Non-Proliferation of Nuclear Weapons (NPT) can be found at Nuclear Threat Initiative (NTI), www.nti.org.

Treaty Overview: The NPT is a multilateral treaty aimed at limiting the spread of nuclear weapons including three elements: (1) non-proliferation, (2) disarmament, and (3) peaceful use of nuclear energy. These elements constitute a "grand bargain" between the five nuclear weapon states and the non-nuclear weapon states.

1. States without nuclear weapons will not acquire them;
2. States with nuclear weapons will pursue disarmament;
3. All states can access nuclear technology for peaceful purposes, under safeguards.

Chapter 5: Electromagnetic superheaters

"Bush and Clinton Visit Haiti," CBC.ca, March 22, 2010.

Mary Anastasia O'Grady, "How the Clintons Worked the Angles in Haiti," *Wall Street Journal*, May 10, 2015. www.wsj.com.

Mark Weisbrot, "Haiti and the International Aid Scam," Guardian, April 22, 2011. www.theguardian.com.

Sean Mallen, "Five Years Later Aid Workers Admit Slow Recovery from Haiti Earthquake," Global News, January 12, 2015. www.globalnews.ca. Veteran aid worker Elvire Douglas said of the earthquake, "It was just like an atomic bomb dropped there."

Transcript, correspondent Tom Foreman and meteorologist Chad Meyers, *The Situation Room with Wolf Blitzer*, CNN, January 13, 2010.

The information on electromagnetic superheaters and particle-beam weapons is not publicly available. Particle-Beam Weapon.

(n.d.). In *Wikipedia*. Retrieved June 24, 2016, from https://en.wikipedia.org/ wiki /Particle-beam_weapon. You might also try reading Particle Accelerator. (n.d.). In *Wikipedia*. Retrieved June 24, 2016, from https://en.wikipedia.org/wiki/ Particle_accelerator.

"More Than 2 Million Affected by Earthquake, Chile's President Says," CNN.com, February 27, 2010.

Alexei Barrioneuvo and Liz Robbins, "1.5 Million Displaced After Chile Quake," *New York Times*, February 27, 2010. www.nytimes.com.

Will Ripley, Junko Ogura and James Griffiths, "Fukushima: Five Years After Japan's Worst Nuclear Disaster," CNN.com, March 11, 2016.

Richard Stone, "Near Miss at Fukushima is a Warning for U.S., Panel Says," *Science Magazine*, May 20, 2016.

Chapter 6: The artificial earthquake

A good summary of the 2004 Indonesian earthquake from John Pickrell, "Facts and Figures: Asian Tsunami Disaster," *New Scientist*, January 20, 2005. www.newscientist.com.

2004 Indian Ocean earthquake and tsunami. (n.d.). In *Wikipedia*. Retrieved June 24, 2016, from https://en.wikipedia.org/wiki/ 2004_Indian_Ocean_earthquake_and_tsunami.

Chapter 7: Russian earthquake recipe

Peter Baker, Michael D. Shear, and David M. Herszenhorn, "Putin Calls Obama to Discuss Ukraine, White House Says," *New York Times*, March 28, 2014.

"5.1-Magnitude Earthquake Hits Huntington Beach," ABC7 News, March 28, 2014.

"2.6-Magnitude Earthquake Hits Huntington Beach," ABC7 News, March 27, 2014.

Jonathan Lloyd, "Magnitude-4.4 Quake Shakes Southern California," NBC4 News, March 17, 2014.

"Ukraine Crisis: Harper Recalls Ambassador, Tells Putin to Withdraw," CBC News, March 1, 2014.

Karen DeYong, "Obama Speaks with Putin by Phone, Calls On Russia to Pull Forces Back to Crimea Bases," *Washington Post*, March 1, 2014.

Ewen MacAskill, Ian Traynor and Dan Roberts, "EU and US Impose Sanctions on Russian and Ukrainian Officials," *Guardian*, March 17, 2014. www.theguardian.com.

"Missing Malaysia Plane MH370: What We Know," BBC, March 7, 2016.

"Malaysia Airlines Flight MH370: What We Know — 2 years later," CBC, March 8, 2016.

Chapter 8: Rise of the climate terrorist

Climate Change articles are everywhere. You can look at "Climate Change," at www.telegraph.co.uk and www.independent.co.uk; try also Jeff Tollefson, "Climate Change: The Case of the Missing Heat," *Nature.com*, January 15, 2014; Tom Clynes, "The Battle Over Climate Science," *Popular Science*, June 21, 2012, www.popsci.com; Larry Bell, "That Scientific Global Warming Consensus...Not!" *Forbes*, July 17, 2012, www.forbes.com.

Chapter 9: The Odyssey of Flight 370

Candace Sutton, "'Planes Don't Just Disappear': Former Malaysian Prime Minister accuses CIA of covering up what really happened to flight MH370," Daily Mail, May 19, 2014. www.dailymail.co.uk.

Boeing company website, www.boeing.com.

"MH17 Malaysia Plane Crash: What We Know," BBC, October 14, 2015.

Agence-France Presse, "MH17 Crash: Dutch Investigators to Assess New Study Implicating Russian Soldiers," *Guardian*, January 4, 2016.

Chapter 10: Overriding pilot controls

Transcript, interview with Brian Todd, *The Situation Room with Wolf Blitzer*, CNN, March 28, 2014. "In 2004, Boeing applied for a system referred to as *uninterruptible autopilot*," said Brian Todd. He went on to explain how ground operators could take control of the plane using radio or satellite signals and steer it to a predetermined airport. They'd be flying it almost like a drone. But the system wasn't hack-proof. Todd added: "Has Boeing advanced this idea from 10 years ago? Has the company still testing it out or has it scrapped the idea entirely? We tried multiple times to get information from Boeing on this project. The company would not speak to us about it."

"E-4 Airborne Command Post," Boeing.com.

The E-4B, dubbed the Doomsday plane, is a military aircraft designed to survive any threat spectrum. "E-4B," U.S. Air Force, September 23, 2015. Retrieved at www.af.mil. "The E-4B is protected against the effects of electromagnetic pulse and has an electrical system designed to support advanced electronics and a wide variety of communications equipment."

"X-37B Orbital Test Vehicle," U.S. Air Force, April 17, 2015. Retrieved at www.af.mil.

Ellie Zolfagharifard and Mark Prigg, "Is the X-37B On a Secret Spy Mission for the US Air Force? Amateur Astronomers Spot Mystery Space Plane in an Unusual Orbit," Dailymail.co.uk, June 2, 2015.

Sellier, C. (Producer), & Conway, J. (Director). (1980). *Hangar 18* [Motion picture]. United States: Sunn Classic Pictures.

Netter, G. (Producer), & Lee, A. (Director). (2012). *Life of Pi* [Motion picture]. United States: 20th Century Fox.

Chapter 11: How to make a plane disappear

CNN Aviation Panel: aviation expert Richard Quest, safety and accident investigator David Soucie, former managing director of the National Transportation Safety Board Peter Goelz, aviation analyst Les Abend, aviation and space journalist Miles O'Brien, aviation lawyer and safety advocate Mary Schiavo, aviation attorney Arthur Rosenberg, and private pilot and science writer Jeff Wise.

Transcript, interview with Jeff Wise, *OutFront*, CNN, March 21, 2014.

Chapter 12: A new covert operation

David Ruppe, "U.S. Military Wanted to Provoke War with Cuba," ABCNews.com, May 1, 2001. America's leadership drafted Operation Northwoods "to trick the American public and the international community into supporting a war to oust Cuba's then new leader, communist Fidel Castro."

"We were wrong, terribly wrong. We owe it to future generations to explain why." R. W. Apple Jr., "McNamara Recalls, and Regrets, Vietnam," *New York Times*, April 9, 1995. In a 1967 memo he wrote to President Johnson, he wrote:

There may be limits beyond which many Americans and much of the world will not permit the United States to go. The picture of the world's greatest superpower killing or seriously injuring 1,000 noncombatants a week, while trying to pound a tiny backward nation into submission on an issue whose merits are hotly disputed, is not a pretty one. It could conceivably produce a costly distortion in the American national consciousness and in the world image of the United States.

Made in the USA
Columbia, SC
21 May 2017